Harvey Rice

Mount Vernon, and Select Poems

Harvey Rice

Mount Vernon, and Select Poems

ISBN/EAN: 9783337317744

Printed in Europe, USA, Canada, Australia, Japan

Cover: Foto ©Thomas Meinert / pixelio.de

More available books at **www.hansebooks.com**

MOUNT VERNON

AND

SELECT POEMS

BY

HARVEY RICE

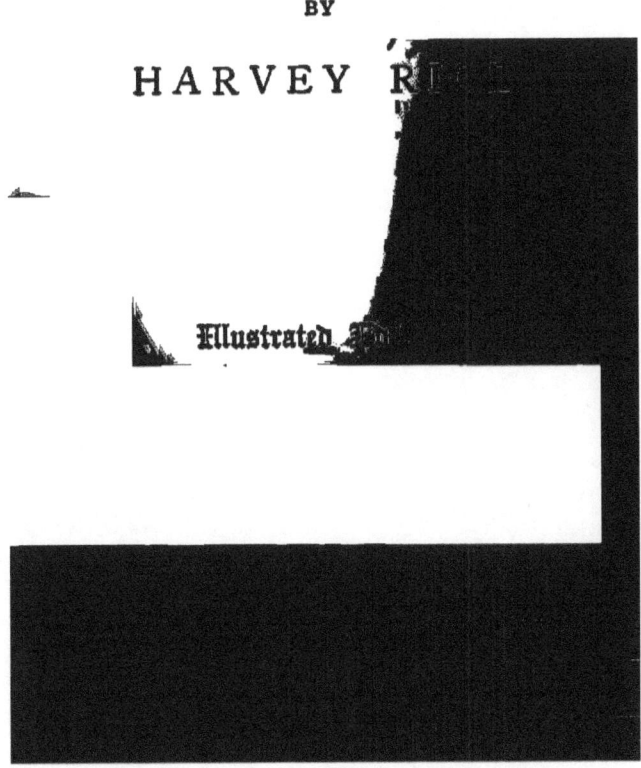

Illustrated

COPYRIGHT, 1882,
BY HARVEY RICE.

CONTENTS.

	PAGE
Mount Vernon	7
Unwritten Music	19
The Moral Hero	21
Footsteps	24
Give us Light	26
Recognition	28
Who is She?	29
The Stream of Time	31
Other Days	33
Morning	38
Warren's Appeal	40
Heaven on Earth	42
The Visionary	43
The Vain Request	45
The Classic Land	47
Song of the Shell	49
Long Ago	51
The Mystery of Life	53
The Celestial Visitant	59
The Voyager	61
Sympathies	63
The Rainbow	65
Departed	67
The Far West	68
Career of the Cloud	71
The Queen of Night	73
The Old Year	75
To a Poetess	76
The Zephyr	78
Hereafter	80

CONTENTS.

	PAGE
A Particular Star	82
Summer	84
Far Away	85
Wild Flowers	86
The Inner Life	88
Voice of the Pine	90
Hymn to the Sun	92
Innocence	95
Enshrined	96
The Birth of Beauty	98
Her Last Adieu	100
Vernal Whispers	102
In Memoriam	104
Song of the Tempest	109
Man	111
Ancestral Portraits	113
The Realm of Thought	122
The Music of the Rain	123
Aspiration	125
Shadows	126
A Vision of Light	129
Laura	131
Song of the Dime	134
The Autumn Leaf	137
Laying the Corner-Stone	139
Inscrutable	141
Ever Vain	142
Tacit Language	143
A Conceit	145
Lilies	147
Home of my Youth	148
More Space	154
Among the Hills	156
Freedom	159
Old Folks' Festival	172
Notes	177

MOUNT VERNON

AND

SELECT POEMS.

MOUNT VERNON.

 On yonder swelling height,
With ivied oaks and cedars crowned,
Where Freedom's banner floats in light,
 And every whispering sound
Breathes of the past, 'tis consecrated ground.[1]

 Pilgrim! ascend the steep,
And there, with true and feeling heart,
On Vernon's brow deep silence keep;
 Ay, let the tear-drop start
While proud yet hallowed thoughts a balm impart.

 Nature hath marked the spot
Where sleeps the great, the good, the wise,
Entombed, yet ne'er to be forgot:
 Ah! there the hero lies,
The man of mighty deeds and high emprise.

 A calm hillside retreat,
Soft mirrored in Potomac's tide,

The spot he chose, at Vernon's seat,
    'Mid wild flowers scattered wide,
And pleasant groves that wave in native pride.

Though but a lowly shrine,[2]
    There grateful hearts delight to pay
Homage to Freedom's son divine,
    The mightiest in the fray,
The mightiest in his country's darkest day.

True worth like his disdains
    The marble's proud emblazoned chart,
And trusts to lore which still remains
    Engraved upon the heart
When crumbling fall the monuments of Art.

But turn where stands the hall[3]
    In which the chieftain dwelt of yore,
And view, still gleaming on the wall,
    The armor which he wore,
With belt and plume, and sabre stained with gore.

Enter with reverent brow
    That old, unguarded mansion proud;
And tread the hearth that's hallowed now,
    Lightly, as you unshroud
The silent past with heart that beats aloud.

And, with the memories dim
　Which gather round that sacred hearth,
　Recall the lessons taught by him
　　Who godlike trod the earth,
And blessed her sons, and gave a nation birth, —

　The patriot calm, yet bold,
　Whose glorious deeds will ever shed
　Renown upon those days of old,
　　When he to battle led
The stern and true who bravely fought and bled.

　'Twas then, in counsels grave,
　That statesmen, noblest of the land,
　Their solemn pledge to Freedom gave,
　　And boldly took their stand
In her defence, united heart and hand.

　And still, unmoved by fear,
　Shall Freedom's sons maintain the right;
　Nor marvel, though the rolling year
　　Disclose to man new light
To cheer his faith, and give him moral might.

　How oft with placid eye
　Has he, whose spirit awes us still,

Stood where we stand, and viewed the sky,
    The river, vale, and hill,
And heard the forest-bird its anthems trill!

And down the vale that sweeps
    In graceful curves to ocean's tide,
How calm the bridal landscape sleeps,
    While zephyrs playful glide,
Fanning the flowers that blush in sinless pride!

And see encircling rise,
    Like sentinels to guard the scene,
Mountains half lost in magic skies,
    With pleasant vales between,
Where Beauty, cradled, wears a smile serene.

Far seen, in all her pride,
    The Federal City lifts her spires,
Where avenues are long and wide,
    And men with large desires
Aspire to place, impelled by patriot fires!

In all her wide domain,
    Say, where has Nature lavished more
To please the eye, the heart to gain,
    Or bid the fancy soar,
Than here upon Potomac's peaceful shore?

MOUNT VERNON.

'Twas here, retired, he sought
  A tranquil life, to love endeared,—
He who the stern resolve had wrought,
  In days of gloom uncheered,
To strike for human rights, though traitors sneered.

And here at eve, I weet,
  Beneath the moonbeam's mellowed ray,
Oft shadowy ranks of warriors meet,
  Who triumphed on that day
When host met host, and heroes carved their way:

Scarred men, in warlike guise,
  Whose hearts still cling to memories dear;
Veterans, whose bosoms heave with sighs
  For him whose bright career
Inspired the oppressed with hope, and kings with fear.

Perchance a stalwart form
  Amid those ranks, high-plumed, is seen,—
Brave Lafayette, who shared the storm,
  Son of a clime serene,
Whose love for Freedom's Land no power could wean.

When last he here surveyed
  His chieftain's tomb in life's frail hour,

How swelled his breast to grief betrayed,
    While tears with magic power [4]
In silence fell, like dewdrops on the flower!

    Nor circumscribe your view,
  But scenes that still surround you greet;
  There rolls Potomac's tide of blue
    Majestic at your feet,
Where busy commerce spreads her whitened sheet.

    In triumph o'er its wave
  Shall ever float our banner's fold,
  While voyagers point the hero's grave,
    And gaze with awe untold
On Vernon's steep, like seer on mount of old.

    And here the garden cheers
  The heart with fruits, and flowers, and shade,
  Where oft, amid eventful years,
    The chief his steps delayed
To share its charms in rich array displayed.

    Even yet, like Eden fair
  Ere innocence beguiled had erred,
  The garden's wealth and balmy air,
    With woman's whispered word,
Enchant the saddened soul that's deeply stirred.

"When Freedom's spirit woke." — Page 13.

When erst the hero drew
His battle-blade amid the wild,
Braddock, to English feeling true,
Spurned him as but a child,
Yet rashly fell with many a victim piled.

Nor dreamed the world as yet
That glittering on a stripling's breast
The "star of empire" had been set;
Nor yet had dreamed the oppressed
How soon that rising star would cheer the West.

When Freedom's spirit woke,
And blood at Lexington had flowed,
Brave men flung off at once the yoke, —
Allegiance long bestowed, —
And flew to arms with zeal that fervent glowed.

From mountain, hill, and glen,
Like torrents rushed the sons of toil, —
Indignant yet high-minded men,
Defenders of the soil,
Whose sturdy blows the oppressor could not foil.

Proud mistress of the sea!
They taught thy pride a lesson wise

Who o'erboard cast rich freights of tea
    Before thy wondering eyes,
And dared thy royal stamp and tax despise.

Though darker grew the day, —
    "A day that tried," as if by fire,
  "Men's souls," — yet heroes led the way,
    Fearless of Britain's ire,
With solemn vow to triumph or expire.

Musing, methinks I hear
  The chieftain's voice, the foeman's tread,
And shout of men who knew not fear,
    Onward to victory led, —
Our brave old sires, with Freedom's banner spread.

Beneath a wintry sky,
  At Trenton, in that glorious fight,
Oh, list the bold, triumphant cry
    Of Liberty and Right,
Flung back from hill to hill with wild delight![5]

'Mid subtle foes combined,
  How firm was he, that gallant one,
Ordained of Heaven to bless mankind, —
    Columbia's noblest son,
The pride of earth, the immortal Washington!

Sternly he led the van,
  The champion of his country's cause,
Sworn to defend the rights of man,
  His country and her laws,
Against a sway that half the world o'erawes.

'Twas he, and he alone,
  Whose skill could guide the banded few, —
The few who shook a monarch's throne, —
  Patriots sore tired, but true;
Those iron men, whose faith still stronger grew.

And well they earned their fame
  Who fixed on Freedom's star their gaze,
And fought and bled in Freedom's name,
  And 'mid the battle's blaze
Bore off the palm, in those heroic days.

Cornwallis! still thy shade
  Bewails, methinks, the fated hour
That saw thee yield thy valiant blade
  A prize to sterner power,
With spirit bowed, till then untaught to cower.

Nor sought he self-renown
  Who scourged the foe, and held the sway;

But now, from proffered kingly crown,[6]
　　With scorn he turned away,
And moral virtue hailed her proudest day.

　　Yet his were honors high, —
　　The highest which the world bestows;
　　And calm, within a peaceful sky,
　　　His star resplendent rose, —
Life's crowning star, triumphant in repose.

　　And peace and plenty reigned, —
　　Still reign to bless the brave and free:
　　While equal rights endeared, maintained,
　　　Have linked in harmony
'he kindred States, which stretch from sea to sea.

　　And yet, though few may dare
　　Columbia's onward march deride,
　　Of power o'ergrown let her beware,
　　　Her glory and her pride,
As onward still she moves with fearless stride.

　　With soul that ne'er repined,
　　He wrought his task, who, great as true,
　　Now bade, with admonitions kind,
　　　To power and place adieu,
\nd, like the Roman, to the plough withdrew.

"And, like the Roman, to the plough withdrew."—Page 16.

MOUNT VERNON.

How vain the lofty tower,[7]
Though reared to heaven by giant hand,
To speak his praise whose matchless power
   Redeemed his native land,
And won him fame that will through time expand!

   On Vernon's rugged side,
Where eagles stoop to build the nest,
There let the hero, with his bride,
   In hallowed slumber rest;
His fittest monument the mountain's crest.

   And there, as they advance,
Let ages yet unborn of time,
Warriors who strike with Freedom's lance,
   And men of every clime,
Revere his dust, and laud his deeds sublime.

   Oh, may the land that's free
Ne'er fall a prey to faction's blight,
But with her glorious history
   Still blend a holier light,
To cheer her sons, and guide them in the right!

   Go fling upon the air,
With bolder hand, her banner's flame;

   And still preserve with jealous care
      Her honor and her fame,
Nor fear to lead the way with heaven-born aim.

   Wide as the world is wide
    Shall freedom's blessings yet extend;
   And man, whate'er his clime, confide
     In man, as friend in friend,
And pride of power her errors wisely mend.

   And sunward still shall soar
    Columbia's eagle bathed in light;
   While yet her sons, schooled in the lore
     Of justice, truth, and right,
Shall worship at her shrine on Vernon's height.

SELECT POEMS.

UNWRITTEN MUSIC.

There's music, music, everywhere,
  Which hills and vales repeat;
Anthems that linger on the air,
  And in the calm retreat.

There's music in the zephyr's sigh,
  And in the breath of flowers,
And in the still small voice that's nigh,
  And in the summer hours.

There's music in the lyric pine,
  And in the rustling leaf,
And in the prayer at holy shrine,
  And in the joy of grief.

There's music in the waterfall,
　　And in the song of bird,
And in the cricket's chirping call,
　　And in a kindly word.

There's music in the surging sea,
　　And in the whispering shell,
And in the wind that's ever free,
　　And in the marriage-bell.

There's music in the bosom's thrill,
　　And in the heart's true beat,
And in the twilight on the hill,
　　And tread of angel-feet.

There's music in the golden spheres,
　　That chant the hymn of time;
And in the bright celestial years,
　　Eternal and sublime.

"There's music in the waterfall." — Page 20.

THE MORAL HERO.

With heart that trusteth still,
  Set high your mark;
And, though with human ill
  The warfare may be dark,
Resolve to conquer, and you will.

Resolve; then onward press,
  Fearless and true:
Believe it, Heaven will bless
  The brave, and still renew
Your hope and courage in distress.

Press on, nor stay to ask
  For friendship's aid:
Deign not to wear a mask,
  Nor wield a coward's blade,
But still persist, though hard the task.

Rest not: inglorious rest
  Unnerves a man.

Struggle: 'tis God's behest.
　Fill up life's little span
With godlike deeds; it is the test, —

Test of the high-born soul
　And lofty aim;
The test in History's scroll
　Of every honored name.
None but the brave shall win the goal.

Go act a hero's part,
　And in the strife
Strike with a hero's heart
　For liberty and life:
Ay, strike for Truth; preserve her chart.

Her chart, unstained, preserve;
　'Twill guide you right:
Press on, and never swerve,
　But keep your armor bright,
And struggle still, with firmer nerve.

Error must fall at last;
　It is ordained:
Old creeds are crumbling fast;
　But, ere the victory's gained,
Heroes must strike, — the die is cast!

What though the tempest rage ;
   Buffet the sea ;
Where duty calls, engage ;
   And, ever striving, be
The moral hero of the age.

FOOTSTEPS.

I HEAR upon the chamber-stair
    Her footsteps light,
Falling like music on the air
    At morn and night.

And oft upon the parlor-floor
    Ingrained with flowers
I hear the step I've heard before
    In happier hours;

And, in the chair that's vacant now,
    Oft think I see
The sainted one with radiant brow
    Who visits me.

Yet when I rise, and turn to greet
    That angel fair,
She disappears, with smile that's sweet,
    Upon the air.

And yet her footsteps oft I hear
    At morn and eve;
And in her whispers, seeming near,
    I still believe,

Nor yield the faith I've cherished long,
    Heartfelt and true,
But, with a hope that still grows strong,
    My faith renew.

In woman's smile, in woman's tear,
    And heart when given,
Star-like there glows a love sincere
    That's born of heaven.

GIVE US LIGHT.

Ay, give us light, more light, to cheer
  Our footsteps onward still:
Welcome the star whose bright career
  Doth fling o'er vale and hill
    Light, — more light!

Methinks I hear the toiling mass,
  Who sweat to pamper pride,
Whisper with murmuring lips, "Alas!
  And why are we denied
    Light, — more light?"

Oh, list! how like the startling wave
  That breaks on Ocean's shore
The voice that wakes the mental slave,
  Who hardly dares implore
    Light, — more light!

True men are they, with lips unsealed,
  Men of unfettered mind,

Who seek the light as 'tis revealed
  In Nature's teachings kind, —
    Light, — more light !

While Truth her glorious banner waves
  From high celestial walls,
Strong men will rise e'en from their graves
To catch the light that falls, —
    Light, — more light !

RECOGNITION.

In the sky afar, afar,
    Where spirits dwell,
I see a lone, lone star,
    And feel its spell.

The holiest star of night,
    Pensive it glows:
I know, by its mild, mild light,
    It shares my woes.

I see, in its saintly smile
    And radiant brow,
A seraph that knows no guile,
    And renew my vow.

WHO IS SHE?

Oh! they say she's the belle of the town:
If you doubt it, I'll wage you a crown
    That ere long you will rue it.
When you meet her, beware! for she can,
If she choose, charm a sensible man,
    'Tis so pleasant to do it!

With the blush of the rose on her cheek,
She affects to be modest and meek:
    Ah! I fear you will rue it.
With the flash of her dark hazel eye
She extorts from the gazer a sigh,
    'Tis so pleasant to do it!

When she flings to the zephyr the fold
Of her scarf, with its purple and gold,
    Look aside, or you'll rue it!
Like a seraph just dropped from the skies,
She attracts by her charms roving eyes,
    'Tis so pleasant to do it!

You may meet her whenever you please,
At the rout, ever gay and at ease;
    But take care, or you'll rue it!
She'll entangle your heart in her smile,
And for mischief she'll tease you a while,
    'Tis so pleasant to do it!

Though enchanting her wit with its spice,
Still her heart is as frigid as ice:
    He who weds her will rue it.
So be careful, nor sigh for the bliss;
Yet you may, if you can, steal a kiss,
    'Tis so pleasant to do it!

But there's danger in taking a sip
From the dewdrop that moistens her lip;
    Who attempts it will rue it:
For in truth she is skilled in her art;
And she boasts, when she breaks a brave heart,
    'Tis so pleasant to do it!

She delights to be weaving a snare,
And to feast on the breath of despair:
    Who disputes it will rue it.
Let her flirt till as old as her aunt,
Then, desiring to wed, find she can't,
    'Tis so *pleasant* to do it!

THE STREAM OF TIME.

It rolls in grandeur lone, —
  The stream of Time;
And on its shores lie strown
  The wrecks of every clime, —

Fragments of ancient art,
  Temples and towers;
And tombs that still impart
  Lessons of life's brief hours.

Yes, empires proud and vast,
  That rose unchecked,
The mightiest of the past,
  Have on that stream been wrecked.

And there, at unknown date,
  Have perished names
Renowned of old and great,
  Plumed lords and jewelled dames.

And, cast like worthless weeds
   Upon the wave,
There cherished hopes and creeds
   Have found a nameless grave.

Yet onward and sublime
   Will ever glide
The silent stream of Time,
   That bears us on its tide.

And we, in turn, shall leave
   Sad wrecks behind, —
The wonders we achieve,
   All save immortal mind.

OTHER DAYS.

THOUGH dear to me are Western charms, —
Rivers and lakes with outstretched arms,
    And prairies broad and free, —
Yet dearer still my native land,
Her mountains, vales, and ocean strand,
With old, tried friends to grasp my hand,
    And welcome me.

Yet mine 'tis not, undimmed, to find
The hearth where glowed affections kind,
    'Mid hopes too bright for tears;
Those purer joys which thrilled my breast,
And gave to life its sweetest zest,
With her whose lip maternal blest
    Mine earliest years!

Still unassailed by ruthless hand,
Oh, let that dear old mansion stand,
    Though strangers tread its hearth!
And spare that elm, unbowed, unbroke,

Which still survives the lightning's stroke,
Crowning the hill, where curls the smoke
    As at my birth.

Not far away, 'mid hillocks green,
The lettered stone, moss-grown, that's seen,
    Watchful o'er sacred dust,
Brings back to me the faded past, —
A mother's love, and kiss, — the last, —
With lessons kind, to which steadfast
    I cling and trust.

With lingering step, and heart sincere,
There let me drop a filial tear,
    In tears still seek relief.
Like Ocean's surge that restless heaves,
My days roll on; yet Memory weaves
Her twilight o'er the past, and leaves
    A balm for grief.

Though mine's a grief no balm can heal,
I love old memories, and still feel
    Their magic o'er me flung.
But list! from steepled church I hear
The old town-clock, deep-toned and clear,
That knells the hours from year to year
    With iron tongue.

And there, adown the vale, I see
A noisy group, low roof, and tree, —
    The spot to which I hied
In summer's heat and winter's snow,
A satchelled lad, who cared to know
Little of books, nor much, I trow,
    That's wise beside.

There glides the brook, whose flowery bank
Was oft the scene of many a prank
    And feat attained at school;
And, like a spectre, near the hill
There stands the same old clicking mill,
Where many an idle urchin still
    Disturbs the pool.

A truant there, beneath the spray
How oft I've angled all the day,
    Or gathered pebbles rare!
Ay, waded half way to the chin
To build the crib, and drive them in, —
The startled brood, with silver fin,
    Shy of the snare.

When woods were tinged with Autumn's hue,
Oft o'er the hills I've brushed the dew,
    Ere flashed the morning's sun,

In search of treasures shaken down
By wind and frost,— nuts white and brown;
Or sought, in chase of game, renown
    With mimic gun.

Around those haunts I loved so well
When but a child there breathes a spell,—
    A spell that charms me yet,—
The stately elm 'neath which I played,
The frowning steep and wizard glade,
And, more than all, the wild cascade
    With jewels set.

And yet there is one hallowed shrine
Around which holier memories twine,—
    Twine with a name that's dear;
The name of one that's sainted now,
The nymph who heard mine earliest vow
With moistened eye, and sunny brow,
    And listening ear.

But where are now those happy years,
Too blest to last, which time endears,
    And faithful hearts embalm?
Those years, the mirthful and the free,
Alas! are lost for aye to me,—
Lost in the past, the dark Dead Sea,
    Where all is calm!

Yet o'er that sea will ever flow
Heart-touching whispers, sweet and low,
    Ay, sanctified to him
Who loves the past, yet hails afar
The seraph Hope, on golden car,
Bearing her lamp, a twinkling star, —
    Twinkling, though dim.

MORNING.

Like a nymph from an ocean of pearls,
    Awaking she flies to the hills,
And smiles at her face and her curls
    As seen in the mirror-like rills.

Her mantle she wove from the mist
    Ere her glittering flight had begun,
And the bracelet that gleams on her wrist
    She wrought from the rays of the sun.

And the diamonds that flash in her hair
    She plucked from the stars of the night;
And, with lips breathing health on the air,
    She kisses the flowers with delight.

And the flowers, clad in purple and gold,
    Her favors return with a smile,
And with love all too pure to be told,
    And with heart that is guiltless of guile.

MORNING.

And, begemmed with the dews of the sky,
    She descends to the silvery lawn,
And surveys with a bright placid eye
    The splendors that glitter at dawn.

And she lingers till awed by her sire,
    Whose eye, burning eye, seems to chide;
Then hastes from his gaze to retire
    With a blush like a beautiful bride;

Yet returns with the dawn of each day,
    Ere her sire re-ascends to his throne,
And, delighted, still sprinkles his way
    With the jewels that flash in her zone.

WARREN'S APPEAL.

[AT BUNKER HILL.]

COMRADES! they come, —
The invaders, fierce and strong!
Hear ye that trump and drum?
They come to do us wrong!
Shall we to tyrant power succumb?

No! calm and still
Await the advancing foe;
And then, with iron will,
Deal death at every blow,
And wrap in lurid flame the hill!

Forsake it not, —
That standard of the free;
Nor let dishonor blot
Its matchless chivalry:
Where'er it waves, defend the spot!

Our country, wives
And children, the strong ties

That bind us, hearts and lives,
Demand that we despise
Danger and death, while hope survives.

Rather than yield,
Let us resolve to die
Upon the battle-field,
Trusting to God on high,
Who is our buckler and our shield.

HEAVEN ON EARTH.

There's a heaven on earth —
   A heaven that's mine —
In the gift of her heart
   Whose love is divine.

There's a light in her eye,
   That wins without art;
And there's grace in her step,
   And joy in her heart.

When the heart blends with heart,
   Confiding and true,
Then on earth there's a heaven,
   With joys ever new.

THE VISIONARY.

A CHILD of genius, — born,
   Not bred in schools, —
He scorns the world's proud scorn,
   Though ranked with fools,
And holds a converse thàt's refined
With Nature, and with Nature's mind.

Nor does he delve with those
   Who delve for gold:
But, rapt in calm repose,
   Like seer of old,
He walks with God the stellar deep,
Where tides of light unbounded sweep;

And wonders why were made
   The earth and stars,
Whose music rolls, unstayed,
   In golden bars;
Nor strives to quench the subtle fire
That wakes his soul to high desire.

Though all that man calls great
   Should he attain,
It would not, could not, sate
   His burning brain;
For he would reach the source of light,
And share, enthroned, the Almighty's might!

Thus lost in thought that's free,
   And manifold,
He ever drifts at sea, —
   Starless and bold;
Yet cannot break the imperial seal
Of fate, nor life's dark myth reveal.

THE VAIN REQUEST.

Give me the heart that's pure and warm,
    Whose virtues constant shine;
Give me the soul that's nobly great,
    Yet melts in grief with mine.

Give me the rosy blushing cheek,
    The lip without a stain;
Give me the meekly pensive eye,
    Whose flash thrills every vein.

Give me the sweet, responsive smile,
    Love's sympathy refined;
Give me an angel's graceful form,
    An angel's sinless mind.

Ay, give me nature, spirit, fire,
    A gem of brilliant ray,
In one who heeds my every wish,
    Though absolute her sway.

Give me but woman thus endowed,
  Whose jewels virtues are,
And I will worship, like a saint,
  So beautiful a star.

But, ah! how vain, how vain, to ask
  A gift so rich and rare,
Since earthly bliss is but a dream,
  And beauty frail as fair!

THE CLASSIC LAND.

Go shroud thee in the mist of olden time,
    Amid the ruins of the past;
Go tread the templed hills of Orient clime,
And list to patriot bards, whose songs sublime
    Inspired, like peal of trumpet blast,
The mountaineers, and woke the slumbering vales,
Ere Greece was heard to pour her funeral wails.

Though fallen, glorious still, O Greece, thy fate! —
    Glorious 'neath centuries of night!
For thine the classic land, the ancient state,
Where sprang the sister arts; and where the great,
    The good, the wise, who sought the right,
Have reared to ages, as they fleetly run,
A proud philosophy, surpassed by none.

But where are now thy beautiful and brave,
    Thy temples, gods, and festal games?

Awe-struck, we trace the isles that gem thy wave,
And point to Athens, and revere thy grave;
  Yes, oft repeat thine honored names
Of heroes, poets, orators, and sage,
And feel thine influence still in every age.

SONG OF THE SHELL.

I was born of the sea,
   And was rocked in its wave,
And its child still would be,
   Though its billows may rave!

For I love to recline
   On the sands of its shore,
Where its smile is divine,
   And terrific its roar!

With a lip that is red
   And as fresh as the dew,
I repeat what is said
   By the ocean to you!

And I bear to the land
   In my bosom a pearl,
A bequest from the strand
   Where the wild waters curl.

'Mid the gems on the breast
  Of the nymph at your side,
Lo, it gleams, ne'er at rest,
  Still a pearl of the tide!

I was born of the sea,
  And was rocked in its wave,
And its child still would be,
  Though its billows may rave!

"When young and gay we climbed the hill and gathered flowers." — Page 51.

LONG AGO.

'Mid pleasant visions gliding dim
    Along the shore,
Where still resounds Life's ocean-hymn
    With solemn roar,
Methinks I see forms tall and slim,
    Angels you know,
Who graced the earth — earth's seraphim —
    Long, long ago.

And in their eyes, as sparkling still
    As in the hours
When young and gay we climbed the hill
    And gathered flowers,
I hail but love and kind good-will,
    And thoughts that glow,
And in my veins still feel the thrill
    Felt long ago.

And, dreaming, hear but whispers sweet,
    From lips unstained,

> The music of the heart's quick beat,
>   That's never feigned;
> And catch a glimpse of twinkling feet
>   'Neath robes of snow, —
> Visions that haunted hall and street
>   Long, long ago.
>
> Oh! is there not a mystic balm
>   In memories old;
> In hopes which still our fears disarm, —
>   Hopes manifold;
> And in the ever-lingering charm
>   Of that sweet woe
> Which grew to love sincere and calm
>   Long, long ago?

THE MYSTERY OF LIFE.

Go trace, O man! thine emanation far
Beyond the bounds of earth. The eldest star
May be thy junior. Ask, nor dare to scan
What was ere uncreated Mind began, —
Yet unbegun, — when heaven itself was dark,
When all was void, and life's ethereal spark
Remained unstruck; nor gaze beyond the verge,
Where thought expires, and silence breathes a dirge!

And yet, in search of truth, why not explore
Divinest realms, — the depths of Nature's lore,
Her prone affinities, her plastic forms,
Her mystic aim, and vital spark that warms
Insensate clay to life, and e'en that part
Which cannot die, the moral sense, the heart?

Whate'er our future fate, remote or near,
Why cherish still a faith that's born of fear?
Or why that crisis view with solemn awe,
The expiring hour ordained by Nature's law, —
Man's last yet glorious birth to life that's higher,
Where love abounds, and pure his soul's desire?

And is it not enough for us to know
That Nature wills our weal, but ne'er our woe?
Then why refuse, amid unclouded light,
To read her lessons, and to choose the right?
Or why still ask, beyond this vale of tears,
If man be blest, or sink the waif of years?
Since life, whate'er its form, whate'er its sphere,
Survives all change, nor stays its bright career.

This planet, Earth, whereon we strive and die,
Compared with mightier orbs that gem the sky,
What is it but a sunbeam's glittering mote?
And what, among the spheres, its lowly note?
And what are systems, with their central sun,
But dazzling lights with which the viewless One
Illumes his boundless realms, and palace-halls,
And hallowed courts that glow with sapphire walls, —
The final home where weary souls shall rest,
And taste but bliss, and be forever blest?

And what is man, with ever-wavering trust?
What but a breathing miracle of dust;
A puzzle to himself, o'er which he sighs,
And questions God, yet thinks himself as wise?
Aspiring still, at most what can he know
Of life not yet revealed 'mid stars that glow?

THE MYSTERY OF LIFE.

Though his an Eden once, it soon became
A scene of tears, and sin acquired a name;
But not till crowned with flowers, and at his side
Angelic woman smiled, and blushed a bride!
Enough, since man was blest, when fatal lore
Touched woman's heart with sorrow to the core,
And placed her in her present sphere, alone,
To cheer the fallen state with love's sweet tone.

Though heirs to grief, we struggle to regain
The treasures of the sky; but, ah! the strain
Which Hope the siren still pours forth misleads
The frantic chase, nor soothes the heart that bleeds;
And yet like shadows, aimless, still we flit,
Perplexed with doubts, nor learn that ills befit
On earth our dark career. 'Tis sweet to think
That we may yet be blest, while link by link
In Nature's chain we climb, and dimly trace
Our destiny, and seize, as if by grace,
E'en on celestial joys; though oft we quake
'Mid ghostly fears, and Wisdom's path forsake.

When Nature counselleth the heart, we hear
Reproving whispers; conscience, or a tear,
Perhaps, betrays us to ourselves; and then
The world, its pride, its pomp, its fools, its men,

Pass huddled in review, — a painful scene,
That sickens life. 'Tis all in vain, I ween,
To ponder o'er the fate of human kind:
All would be happy, yet all will be blind.

Ah! why do men still seek it as a prize, —
The happiness which dazzles envious eyes, —
And yet forget the source of moral good,
The charities of life, least understood?
Why penetrate the mountain's rocky side
For crumbs of gold, or track the ocean wide
To gather pearls, and, at some future day,
Expect to bask beneath the sunny ray
Of earthly bliss, yet die at last the slaves
Of Folly's reign, and fill forgotten graves?

Forbear the human bosom to unmask:
The passions prompt us, whatsoe'er we ask;
And Virtue's path, though traced upon a chart,
We seldom choose till grief refines the heart.
Yet hope links heaven and earth; and thus, despite
The human will, unerring Nature's light
Constrains belief, and teaches that the soul
Must be immortal. Nor can aught control
This innate sense. Alas! who would persuade
Himself, by dint of lore or logic's aid,

That dark annihilation, cheerless creed,
Ingulfs us all at last, then blots the deed?

Though man may seem, with his restricted powers,
The victim still of Fortune's freakish hours,
Yet rule he may — and overrule — by thought
Which still expands, till he himself is wrought
To more than man. And when, at last, the breath
Which he inhales at birth departs at death,
He but attains to life, — a soul refined,
That's merged again in elemental Mind.

Oft from the darkened past, as from an urn,
The memories dear of those we loved return,
And tell of days and years and feeling hearts,
When friendship knew but truth, and love no arts;
When joys were pure, and in life's golden sky
No darkling cloud arose to blind the eye;
When Hope with smiling brow inspired the hours,
And earth seemed but a paradise of flowers.

Amid the gloom of years old empires rest;
And who can say if they were cursed or blest?
The monuments which told with lettered trust
Where slept the great have crumbled into dust.
Perchance the clods on which we heedless tread
Have breathed with life, — the ashes of the dead, —

Ashes which yet shall wake to conscious life,
And, in the great advancing drama's strife,
Assume, with new-born joy and purer heart,
Still higher forms, and play a nobler part.
And yet why doubt, or yield to mystic fear?
What Nature wills, God wills, — a truth that's clear.

THE CELESTIAL VISITANT.

LIKE the ray of a lone bright star
   Her spirit oft visits me still,
And brings back the years from afar
   When heart beat to heart with a thrill.

And, tinting my dreams with the hue
   Of a smile derived from the sky,
She moistens my brow with the dew
   Of a tear-drop warm from her eye.

And sweetly she breathes in my ear
   . The vow which I made in my youth,
And with lips still fervid and dear
   She pledges her love and her truth.

And in tones still gentle and kind
   She whispers of joys that are past, —
Of life, with its pleasures refined;
   And of love's first dream, and its last.

And arrayed like a bride crowned with flowers,
   Though life's early dream hath departed,
Beyond the dark cloud that still lowers
   She awaits me, my own true-hearted.

THE VOYAGER.

When burst that thrilling cry
Of "Land-ho!" on the voyager's ear,
With what delight his searching eye
Beheld the shadowy mountains lie
    Far in the distance, — dim, yet clear!

A world before him lay
In all its beauty and its prime:
With fearless step he led the way,
And knelt on shore, and blessed the day,
    The most eventful of his time.

Freely the golden land,
That gave a tint to all his dreams,
Yielded to him, with heart and hand,
Her empire vast, from strand to strand,
    With all her wealth of hills and streams.

But Nature's children then
Dreamed not of woes which time revealed:

They saw but gods in Europe's men,
And still revered them, even when
   Their fate had been forever sealed.

And yet that wiser Power,
Who shapes the destiny of man,
Had willed a brighter, happier hour
To cheer the gloom, which seemed to lower
   In darkness o'er his moral plan.

And with the years which came
There came brave men, whose valor won
For Freedom's land a glorious name,
And on whose altar burns the flame
   That once inspired a Washington.

Intenser let it burn, —
The flame that still inspires the free, —
Till man the rights of man shall learn,
And every land become, in turn,
   A glorious land of liberty!

SYMPATHIES.

I LOVE to think that spirits dwell
Upon the earth, — the beautiful, the good,
Whose sympathies are pure, yet understood
    By none save those who feel the spell.

I love to think that in life's vale
There are ungathered flowers, whose bosoms glow
With silent feeling and with tender woe
    For him whose hopes, long cherished, fail.

I love to think that still a ray,
Divine like that of hope, will long be felt
By her to whom in earlier years I knelt, —
    The vision of my darkened way.

I love to think that golden hours
Will yet be mine while here on earth I tread, —
Blest hours, when fairer skies will glow o'erhead,
    And nought spring 'neath my feet but flowers.

I love to think that I shall meet,
In holier realms, the dear departed few, —
Angelic souls affectionate and true,
    Whose last kind words I oft repeat.

I love to think that I shall read
The record of His mighty plan divine
Who dwells in light, and in each golden line
    Acquire the wisdom which I need.

I love to think that I shall reign
In some bright sphere, with power to tread the way
From star to star through life's eternal day,
    And still to higher spheres attain.

THE RAINBOW.

How beautiful to wondering eyes
   The rainbow's flame,
That spans the earth, and tints the skies,
   Hallowed in name,
And blent with more than Tyrian dyes!

How like bright hopes its glories shine,
   Distant, yet nigh!
Its woven hues, oh, how divine!
   Though doomed to die
In fitful mood, like hopes of mine.

And yet within the heavenly gate
   Its smiles invite
Earth's weary pilgrim, child of Fate,
   To share the light
Which death nor gloom can dissipate.

It cheers the faith to which we cling,—
   Faith in the dream

Of life, and in the hopes that fling
    Earthward a gleam
Of heaven, like flash of angel's wing.

Emblem of love and power untold,
    It crowns His brow
Who doth the skies about him fold,
    Keeping his vow,
And golden promise made of old.

DEPARTED.

Too pure for earth, too pure for earth,
    Thy home the spirit-land,
Where earth-born flowers unfading smile,
    Transferred by angel hand!

Yes, on thy brow the calm, bright skies
    Of heaven their radiance shed:
The gift is thine, an angel's harp.
    How blest the early dead!

From sorrow's vale uncheered and dark,
    From tears and vain desires,
While young and sinless thou art freed,
    The soul to heaven aspires.

But still thy name remains intwined
    With memories ever dear,
And they who on thee oft have smiled
    Now smile but through a tear.

THE FAR WEST.

Oh, where, think ye, is now the West,
   The far, far West, the land of dreams,
Whose hills and vales, with virgin breast,
Still slumber in their ancient rest,
   Lulled by the voice of plaintive streams?

From Mexico, where airs are bland,
   To Oregon's impetuous flood,
Already vale and mountain land
Resound to that advancing band
   Who proudly boast heroic blood.

Nor distant is the day, perchance,
   When yet these sons of valiant sires
Shall win their way by love or lance
To sunnier climes, and e'en advance
   Beyond the equator's solar fires.

Thus race to race must ever yield,
   And mental power assume the sway:

THE FAR WEST.

Broad as the earth the ample field
For those who trust in Virtue's shield,
   And Freedom's banner dare display.

The far, far West, 'tis Freedom's now,
   The gift of God to earth's oppressed, —
The land where all who take the vow
No more to king or priest to bow
   May come, and find their wrongs redressed.

Ay, there shall happy millions yet
   Reclaim the soil, and crowd the mart, —
Freemen who thrive by toil and sweat,
Sprinkling the waste with cities set
   On hill and plain like gems of art.

And there shall thought yet fly afar
   Along the wire, from climes remote,
And blend with thought like star with star;
While startling rolls the frantic car,
   And bannered glides the gallant boat.

And there, unawed, the mind of man,
   Progressive still, shall still aspire,
Nor yield to creeds that fear to scan
The mystic lore of Nature's plan,
   But still, insatiate, aim the higher!

In sooth it needs no prophet's eye
   Westward to Ocean's calmer surge
To see the future there outvie
The ancient world, whose glories lie
   Pillared on Time's receding verge.

Oh! what, when centuries have rolled,
   Will be this mighty Western land?
Her sons — will they be brave and bold,
And still defend her banner's fold?
   Her holy altars — will they stand?

The link that binds the sisterhood —
   Say, will it brighten and grow strong,
And men bear rule, the great and good,
Who shun dissension, strife, and blood,
   Yet cleave to right, nor yield to wrong?

Fear not! with holier influence yet
   The years shall come which God ordains;
When Freedom's bounds shall not be set,
Nor man his fellow-man forget
   In blind pursuit of sordid gains.

CAREER OF THE CLOUD.

In the garb of a soft, silken mist,
   I ascend to the brow
Of the mountain, and trust to my wings
   When expanded as now.

And I darken the sky with a frown
   That is fearful and grim;
And, encircled with fire flashing wild,
   Often mutter a hymn —

With a harmony solemn and loud,
   And with power that appalls,
As it rolls its dread echoes afar
   Through the sky's vaulted halls!

Yet, relenting, I cheer the parched earth,
   And refresh it with showers,
And awake thrills of joy in the breast
   Of the grief-stricken flowers.

Though away like a shadow I pass,
    Still I feel a desire
To repose in the smiles of the sun,
    Clad in robes fringed with fire;

But in sorrow return to the earth,
    In whose clime I was born,
And in silence await the calm light
    Of the beautiful morn!

THE QUEEN OF NIGHT.

PALE wanderer in the azure field
   That blossometh with stars,
Why guard thy breast with silver shield,
   Whose dreams no sorrow mars?
And why so fickle in thy round
Through realms celestial and profound?

And why, with ever-smiling face,
   O'er golden pathways lone,
Dost thou at eve delight to chase
   Dim shadows, all thine own,
Yet beautiful, and lovely too,
As rosy nymphs that brush the dew?

And why in thine employ retain
   That archer ever bold
Who aims at maiden and at swain
   His arrows tipped with gold,
Yet strives to soothe, with winning art
And holiest vow, the wounded heart?

Empress of Love! 'tis ever thine
   To wield a magic power,
That's earthly half, and half divine;
   And thine the witching hour
When pledges sweet are often given,
Yet only true when sealed in heaven.

THE OLD YEAR.

Lo! the Year now retires,
The sad Old Year, like a king from his throne;
And, fated, he sinks, unwept and alone,
　　To the grave of his sires.

Yet he bears in his hand
A scroll of sweet memories traced with a tear, —
Thoughts which come back to the heart like a seer
　　From the dark Silent Land.

The decrees of his reign
Enshrined let us cherish, though summoned to part
With friends whom we loved, the wealth of the heart,
　　In the vale of the slain.

Yet we sigh for the years
Which Hope has begemmed with promises bright,
And wait, though they come not, save with the night
　　Of the grave and with tears.

TO A POETESS.

Swan of the sweet and pensive song,
  Forgive this proffered lay:
Though envied by a rival throng,
  Aspire! and win thy way
To every heart that loves delight.
  Traced on the scroll of Fame,
  Already thine's a name
That, brightening, sheds a stellar light.

Fear not! but trust to bolder wing,
  And, in a trackless sky,
Ascend 'mid stars, whose anthems fling
  Still back a sweet reply.
Aspire! nor heed the critic's blast,
  But still with many a gem
  Enrich thy diadem;
And pour thy strains, and they shall last.

Yes, warbler of our Western land,
  The destiny is thine

Among the gifted few to stand,
  A favorite of the Nine.
Aspire! and o'er Time's ocean-tide
  Still loftier strike thy lyre;
  Strike it, with soul of fire,
To notes that wake a nation's pride.

THE ZEPHYR.

BORN of the air,
Say, whither, whither, dost thou glide,
With breath of balm, on azure tide,
    Viewless, yet fair?

O'er hill and dale
'Tis thine to stray, and share the smile
Of stars and flowers, and without guile
    Thyself regale.

At summer eve,
On gentle wing that fans my brow,
Why stoop, or, blandly whispering now,
    Ask why I grieve, —

Grieve for the blest,
The dearly-loved one, now no more,
To whom an angel oped the door
    In realms of rest?

Yet, when I hear
The loving whisper of thy lute,
I think it hers whose lip is mute,
    And hope and fear;

And, though in vain,
Still wait to hear one whisper more,
And still at Beauty's shrine adore,
    Nor would refrain.

Her spirit, bright
And seraph-like, looks down from heaven;
While I look up with soul unshriven,
    And hail the light.

HEREAFTER.

Alas! how fearful, silent, vast,
   The dim and shadowy realm
Where undisputed reigns the Past,
   And voiceless waves o'erwhelm,
In dark Oblivion's darker tide,
All that we are, with all our pride,
   Lost in the dread Hereafter!

And will there be no whisper heard,
   No voices kind and sweet,
No tender heart-string touched or stirred,
   No love that is complete,
To soothe the grief that cannot speak;
No faithful friend, tear-eyed and meek,—
   None in the dread Hereafter?

And will there be no more of earth,
   No more of sky and stars,
No hills or vales, nor vernal birth
   Of flowers, nor radiant bars

HEREAFTER.

Of light to break upon the stream
That bears us onward like a dream, —
  On, — in the dread Hereafter?

Believe, there is no death for him
  Who lives on earth aright:
He sees no shadows dark or grim;
  For him there is no night,
No last dull sleep, no fearful knell,
Nor terror, when he goes to dwell,
  Blest, in the dread Hereafter.

A PARTICULAR STAR.

O'er the mountain, the hill, and the vale,
   When the gems of the night gleam afar,
Say, who turns not with rapture to hail,
   High enthroned, a particular star?

Though too fondly of bliss we may dream,
   And though sorrows our happiness mar,
Still who loves not to bask in the beam
   Of a bright yet particular star?

Who that dwells 'neath the musical spheres,
   Chiming low without quaver or bar,
Can resist the sweet smiles or the tears
   Of a very particular star?

Yes, as pure as the smile in the sky,
   When the Morning appears on her car,
Is the love-light that gleams in the eye
   Of a dear yet particular star!

May he find her the charm of his life,
   Ever kind without discord or jar,
Who, enraptured, has won for a wife
   An adored yet *particular* star!

SUMMER.

Lo! Summer sérenely advances,
   Arrayed in the smiles of the sun;
While zephyrs are weaving their dances
   In the vales where the rivulets run;
And notes from the woodland soothingly steal
The heart that is wounded, — never to heal.

When alone, — a recluse in the bower, —
   Communion with Nature how sweet!
Her whispers and smiles have the power,
   'Mid the charms of her fairy retreat,
To recall the blest hours whose flight we bemoan,
And awake in the soul a heaven of its own.

Though Summer ere long with her pleasures
   Must yield to the cold Winter blast,
And we who are fed from her treasures
   Depart, and be lost in the past;
Yet hope, like a star still unclouded and bright,
Dispels every fear, and illumines the night.

FAR AWAY.

Is there not a domain whose broad, sunny fields
   Are begemmed with perennial flowers,
Far away in a realm of beauty and song,
   Where but joy, unrepressed, speeds the hours?

If there be such a realm of fairy delight
   With an atmosphere laden with balm,
Be it mine there to dwell, where from innocent lips
   Breathes a music like that of a psalm.

Though divine be the star that illumines our way,
   We are plodding a path set with snares;
And the life that we lead is a warfare indeed,
   And its pleasures but cankering cares.

How blest then to fly from this sorrowing vale
   Far away to the bright happy land,—
The beautiful land where life is but love,
   And the smiles that await us are bland!

WILD FLOWERS.

Daughters of light, who ne'er repine,
    Though high your birth,
'Tis yours in humble life to shine
    Like modest worth.

Arrayed in robes of heavenly hue
    You come and go,
And drink the nectar of the dew,
    Nor taste of woe.

Inspired, and yet inspiring still,
    You seem to speak,
And prophesy to vale and hill
    With faith that's meek.

'Tis yours a language pure to teach,
    And share his heart
Who seeks on earth high aims to reach
    Ere he depart.

And yours the whisper which, I trow,
    I hear at eve,
And in the morning's roseate glow, —
    Hear and believe;

Believe the gospel of your lips
    Spoken to man,
Nor heed the coming frost that nips
    Each hope and plan.

For, if my life on earth be true,
    I yet, on high,
Shall wear a glorious robe like you,
    And never die.

THE INNER LIFE.

Go forth, deep lost in thought,
   Where none intrude,
And let thy faith be wrought
   In solitude :
Truth waits, yet must be sought.

Yes, with thyself commune,
   And, soft as lute,
Thy heart-strings thus attune
   To love that's mute,
And vain aspirings prune.

'Tis only love — complete —
   That will endure,
When earth-life frail and fleet,
   And hopes not sure,
Depart, — pure love, I weet, —

The sentiment that's shrined
   Deep in the heart;

The wealth of soul and mind;
   That better part
Of man, not yet defined.

The life of life upright,
   God-like endeavor;
The star that crowns the night;
   The long forever
That's lost in calm delight.

VOICE OF THE PINE.

In other days, from woodland maze,
   Homeward I proudly bore,
O'er hill and plain, 'mid sleet and rain,
The graceful pine that breathes divine
   Its music at my door.

There let it stand, pride of the land,
   And in my listening ear
Still breathe its psalm, low-voiced and calm;
Sad notes of grief — in my belief —
   Which angels stoop to hear.

I feel its power at twilight-hour,
   And think that she is near
Who reigns afar in yonder star, —
A seraph blest, her soul at rest,
   The brightest of her sphere.

How dear to me the whispering tree,
   Whose sigh melts on the air! —

Sweeter than words, or song of birds;
Because its tone is like her own
  Sweet voice, lute-like and rare.

Long be it mine, beneath that pine,
  To dream of years gone by;
Of her who seems, in all my dreams,
To visit earth, where love had birth, —
  A love too pure to die.

HYMN TO THE SUN.

Great sire of life, and source of light,
    Thou hast o'er all control;
Dispeller of the mystic night,
    Of worlds the central soul.

Shot from thy quiver, swiftly fly,
    Space-wide, thine arrowy rays;
Falling, like fire-flakes from the sky,
    Into the boundless maze.

The sinless stars, so bright and fair,
    Are all allied to thee;
Daughters of heaven, with golden hair,
    That smile o'er land and sea.

From thee the Earth her wealth receives,
    Her beauty, fruits, and flowers;
And at thy nod old Ocean heaves,
    And feels thy quickening powers.

Yes, all that live, from thee partake
    A life that never dies, —
A life that sleeps but to awake
    In life beyond the skies.

And they who worship in thy name,
    And share thy gifts of fire,
Still in thy smiling face of flame
    Behold creation's Sire, —

The lofty One, whose outline dim
    Pervades, unseen, the vast;
The realm that's sanctified by Him,
    The mighty First and Last.

Oh that we could unveil to sight
    The depths of Nature's plan, —
The infinite in power and might,
    Whose crowning work is man!

Although the seal we cannot break,
    Yet, blest with godlike powers,
Why not, at least, ourselves forsake,
    And scale the loftiest towers? —

The pinnacles that gleam on high
In that unchanging clime
Where ne'er is heard an earthly sigh,
Nor lisp that breathes of time.

INNOCENCE.

How can a soul of sinless ray,
Now breathing love, incline to stray,
    Or need to be forgiven?
O Innocence, with laughing eyes!
Thou art a cherub from the skies,
    A wanderer from heaven.

Ha! gentle spirit, gift divine,
There's nectar on those lips of thine,
    And sweet the kiss I've won:
There dwells no dew on proffered lip,
That's pure, like that on thine, to sip, —
    On loveliest woman's, — none.

With heart sincere, while it shall beat,
May violets spring beneath thy feet,
    And roses crown thy youth;
And, when to womanhood attained,
Still may thy graces be unfeigned,
    Thy friendship, love, and truth!

ENSHRINED.

From crystal fount in yonder sky
    A silvery dewdrop fell, —
Fell, like a tear from Beauty's eye,
    Into the flowery dell.

And there, amid the starlight's tide,
    I plucked the floweret wild,
Into whose breast, with loving pride,
    The dewdrop fell and smiled, —

A smile that slept enshrined within
    That glittering drop of dew;
Yet seemed a spirit without sin,
    Whose life, though brief, was true;

Spirit that kissed the floweret fair,
    And woke within its breast
A love which Nature bids us share,
    Serene, angelic, blest.

ENSHRINED.

How oft in nature thus we see,
  Mirrored as in a glass,
A life of love and purity,
  Which we unheeding pass!

In every drop of sparkling dew,
  In every smiling flower,
There is a lesson meant for you
  And me, — a voice of power;

A voice that speaks to every heart,
  In silence mute yet bland;
That wins the soul with mystic art,
  Like a dream in the blissful land.

THE BIRTH OF BEAUTY.

By Nature's hand, though all
   Was made complete,
Still in her palace-hall
   No twinkling feet,
Nor graceful figure tall,
   Nor smile that's sweet,
Had yet obeyed her call.

And so she racked her brain,
   And gathered flowers, —
White lilies from the plain,
   And from the bowers
Roses, — and from the main
   Cosmetic powers;
From birds, their sweetest strain.

Combining these, she wrought
   A perfect charm;
And gave it grace and thought,

Brilliant yet calm;
When man the vision caught
In his strong arm,
And claimed it, — as he ought! —

And blessed his happy lot,
Which now made earth
An Eden, — every spot, —
Since Beauty's birth;
Whose smile still cheers his cot,
His home and hearth;
An angel — is she not?

HER LAST ADIEU.

Adieu to him who loved me not;
   Whose vow was insincere:
The past — oh, let it be forgot,
   With all on earth that's dear!

The Silent Land — it is my home;
   And there I soon shall rest,
Where sorrows never, never come
   With sighs to heave the breast.

Adieu to earth! When I am laid
   Within the narrow cell,
Let words and funeral pomp be stayed,
   Nor toll the funeral-bell.

Enough if but a friend be nigh
   To fling upon my bier
A rose that's tinted with the sky,
   Or shed for me a tear.

HER LAST ADIEU.

Speak not of cherished love untold,
  In death, a deathless flame;
Nor let the marble pale and cold
  Record my humble name.

Yet think of me whene'er you dream
  In holy twilight-hours,
Or mark the star whose pensive beam
  Still cheers the meek-eyed flowers.

VERNAL WHISPERS.

Born of the blushing Spring,
Lo, Joy replumes his angel-wing!
With radiant locks the Hours advance,
And violets wake from Winter's trance;
While Beauty smiles with sunny glance,
    And birds ecstatic sing.

Against a sky serene
The quiet mountains seem to lean;
While valleys woo, with pure delight,
The genial sun, and dews of night;
And Hope, with buds of promise bright,
    Embroiders all the scene.

The sunshine and the showers
Restore to Earth her bosom flowers, —
The queenly rose that's virgin-lipped,
The lily that in gold is dipped,
The honey-bell that's oftenest sipped,
    And thyme that never towers.

And now, from mantled hill,
And cradled vale, and gushing rill,
There breathes a music sweet and long,
Which melts the soul like sacred song,
And purifies the heart that's wrong, —
  The whisper small and still.

Oh! catch with listening ear
The vernal whispers of the year,
Whose breath, like hope, revives the heart,
And bids us act a nobler part,
Nor leave behind a faithless chart
  When Autumn's leaf is sear.

IN MEMORIAM.

The stars were bright as at their birth,
   And angel-voices thrilled the air;
   When, spirit-like, and pure as fair,
She came to bless our home on earth.

Her new-born life, like budding flower,
   Awoke as from the slumbering night,
   And smiled to greet the morning light,
And grew in love and artless power.

And, with the lapse of speeding years,
   She grew in graces which adorn
   The woman, lovely as the morn,
And beautiful 'mid hopes and fears.

With modest mien, enchanting all,
   She seemed a vision from the sky,
   The cynosure of every eye
In social sphere or festive hall.

Yet higher aims in life she sought,
   And early chose that "better part,"
   God's love, which purifies the heart
When in the soul 'tis deeply wrought.

Her smile was like a magic charm,
   A heavenly twilight blandly wove;
   And in an atmosphere of love
She ever moved serene and calm.

In Fashion's glare, or humbler sphere,
   Wherever souls have genial flow,
   Admirers paused, and whispered low
Her praise in words which were sincere.

And one there was, a man of heart,
   Of finest feelings, kind, yet brave,
   To whom her jewelled hand she gave;
Ay, gave her life, of his a part.

And theirs was now a cloudless sky,
   With pleasing hopes and noble pride;
   For they were one, bridegroom and bride,
Nor dreamed that aught could break the tie.

On rapturous wing the blest hours flew,
   With joys renewed as sped the day;
   And vernal flowers smiled on the way,
And mountain-scenes entranced the view.

Nor long awaiting their return,
   Friends welcomed them with earnest kiss,
   The purest, holiest earthly bliss,
In homes where sacred altars burn.

How joyous now the festive hour,
   When music cheered the lighted hall,
   And wreaths of flowers bedecked the wall,
And Beauty smiled with witching power!

Yet many days passed not away
   Ere on their path a shadow fell,
   Whose mystic meaning none could tell, —
A shadow that prolonged its stay.

Full soon the final summons came,
   And o'er the River dark and wide
   Forever passed the sainted bride,
Whose love still lives, a deathless flame.

And he whose love had won her heart,
   And they who shared its kindred ties,
   Bemoaned her flight with tearful eyes,
And bosoms pierced by Sorrow's dart.

Where now her dust in silence sleeps,
   There oft a footstep light is heard;
   And there as oft his soul is stirred
Who truly loved, and, loving, weeps.

There autumn sheds the faded leaf
   Upon that hallowed spot of earth,
   And there the vernal flower has birth,
Emblems of her whose life was brief.

There was she laid, with tender care,
   In bridal robes, — her last request, —
   The weary one now gone to rest,
The loved, the beautiful, the fair!

Ah! must it be? — must we no more
   On earth behold her happy face,
   Her loving smile, and queenly grace,
Nor hear her steps within our door?

How oft she touched to pensive song
   The melting strings of her guitar, —
   Melting, like music from afar,
In tones that linger, sweet and long!

Oh, how endeared each relic seems
   Which she has left behind to tell
   Of her sweet self, and which, like spell,
Recalls her still in pleasing dreams!

SONG OF THE TEMPEST.

CLOUD-BORN, I visit earth,
   And on my way sublime
I give to terror birth,
   Nor spare the sons of time,
But in my wrath sweep o'er the land,
And smite my foes with giant hand.

Oh, yes! with fearful stroke
   I smite the forest's pride,
Uproot the stately oak,
   And score the mountain's side,
And dash to earth, in frenzied hour,
The abodes of men, with fane and tower.

O'er land and sea I sweep,
   Unchained in mad career,
Nor list to those who weep,
   But hurl the lightning's spear;
And, wrapped in clouds that still grow black,
Still scatter wrecks along my track.

And thus, with crushing stride,
   I leave a record lone
Of sorrow and of pride,
   Nor care my deeds to own;
For passion fires my giddy brain
Until exhaustion ends my reign.

But still — if understood —
   I do but fill my sphere;
Educe from evil good,
   And mark the fruitful year:
Yet man distrusts the hand concealed
That points my path o'er flood and field.

MAN.

What a mystical vision is he,
   In a "house" built of "clay," —
Haunted house that is locked with a key,
   And the "key" thrown away!

What a mystical vision is he,
   With his heart in a "chest,"
And a "hinge" in his suppliant knee,
   And a "sole" ne'er at rest!

What a mystical vision is he,
   With a "drum" in his ear,
And a "font" in his eye ever free
   To o'erflow with a tear!

What a mystical vision is he,
   With a "palm" in his hand,
And the "lines" of his fate as you see, —
   Still the "lord" of the land!

What a mystical vision is he,
    With a "pipe" in his throat,—
Often piping a song of glee,
    Or a sad, sad note!

What a mystical vision is he,
    With his hands and his feet
Pierced with "nails" by a natal decree,
    And a "beard" like the wheat!

What a mystical vision is he
    When a "lid" shuts his eye,
And his "ghost" pays to Charon a fee
    That is stamped with a "die"!

What a mystical vision is he,
    Whether living or dead!
Still a man, or a god it may be,
    With a "crown" on his head.

ANCESTRAL PORTRAITS.

WITH all their virtues plain and stern,
   The good old times have sped;
And now the wisdom which we learn
   Turns giddy every head:
And yet 'tis wrong, I ween, to spurn
   Our old ancestral dead.

Our Pilgrim sires were taught of God,
   And solemn psalms they sung:
They trained their children with the rod,
   And witch and wizard hung.
Yet, if they erred, 'tis nothing odd:
   All err, both old and young.

They earned by toil whate'er they had,
   Since Heaven ordained it so;
Nor with the fashions went they mad,
   Nor cramped they waist or toe;
Nor like the lily, pale and sad,
   Looked every belle and beau.

The girls were taught to spin and weave,
   The boys to hold the plough:
'Twas then thought wise — and I believe
   As wise it might be now —
If people would their scheming leave,
   And live by sweat of brow.

The good old times were good enough,
   Though times more polished dawn:
Men then were made of sterner stuff
   Than those that now are born.
Though plain they were, and somewhat rough
   Yet why their virtues scorn?

In groups that grace the parlor wall,
   How pleasant still to see
The dear old portraits, which recall
   Our honored ancestry! —
Grandparents, uncles, aunts, and all,
   Who danced us on the knee.

Oh, yes! I still remember well
   My grandsire's aged look;
The witching tales he deigned to tell;
   And how from sacred Book
He oft explained why Adam fell,
   And man the right forsook.

He used to wear a broad-brimmed hat;
   A buckle gemmed each knee.
The old arm-chair in which he sat
   It cheers me still to see:
With powdered wig and cue, all that,
   None looked so grave as he.

His was a high and manly brow,
   With locks of silver gray:
He ne'er to Britain's pride would bow,
   Nor for her king e'en pray;
Nor would he yield, like statesmen now,
   His principles for pay.

But, strong of limb, and brave at heart,
   He swung a brawny arm,
And promptly bore a hero's part
   'Mid danger and alarm;
And, though oft pierced by Sorrow's dart,
   His manner still was calm.

He loved to tell his history o'er,
   And speak of War's dread crimes,
And laud the deeds he did of yore,
   Which beat all modern times.
The worldly goods he left in store
   All heirs could ask, save dimes!

Though poor, he was a patriot true;
    Had fought in Freedom's cause;
And all he owed he paid when due, —
    His debt to Nature's laws:
In fact, from earth have passed but few
    With heart as free from flaws.

If 'midst old graves you choose to tramp,
    You still may read in print,
Upon his headstone cold and damp,
    This brief yet truthful hint:'—
"Here lies a man of Nature's stamp,
    The coinage of her mint."

But what of her who wore a cap,
    And hoop to swell her skirt? —
Dear grandam, who with many a chap,
    When young, inclined to flirt;
And e'en in age, whate'er might hap,
    Seemed girlish, prim, and pert.

Though seeming gay, she used to read
    Her Bible with delight,
And deeply felt that mortals need
    God's grace to keep them right:
Always, with heart that seemed to bleed,
    She said her prayers at night.

She led a life none need despise,
   Affectionate and kind;
And, under holy guidance wise,
   Her duty sought to find;
And oft relieved, with pitying eyes,
   The poor, the halt, the blind.

Her fears were still her only foes,
   Her aim but heaven to win;
Yet she was cheerful to life's close,
   Though but a shadow thin;
Oft rocked my cradle, I suppose;
   And loved to knit and spin.

The most I recollect of her
   Is, how she used to try,
With pointed thread half lost in blur,
   To hit her needle's eye;
And, though vexations would occur,
   She ne'er indulged a sigh.

The good old lady has been dead
   Some thirty years at least:
The stone is carved, that guards her head,
   With cherubs gazing east;
And yet she lives, though life hath sped,
   Where all her fears have ceased.

Uncle, who was a favorite son,
   For riches never toiled:
Though he in youth loved mirth and fun,
   And sports that oft recoiled,
Yet what was wrong he aimed to shun,
   And ne'er his morals soiled.

But, when parental power had lost
   O'er him its kind control,
He rarely stopped to count the cost,
   The worth of time or soul,
But onward floated, tempest-tost,
   Where'er Life's wave might roll.

His head with many a vision swam:
   The world he longed to see;
Or Greenland's isle, or land of Ham,
   It mattered not, so he,
No longer tethered like the lamb,
   Could rove unchecked and free.

Ere twenty-one, most foreign lands
   'Tis said that he had seen.
Though fearful still of wedlock's bands,
   At forty, as I ween,
He sometimes thought of joining hands:
   What did the fellow mean?

However strange, the truth to say,
    Love's vow at last he made,
And sealed it too, one eve in May,
    With her who graced the glade;
And ever, from that happy day,
    He led a life that's staid.

Whate'er may be by prudes required,
    Who join in nuptial state,
He proved the model man desired,
    And she the loving mate;
And, blest of Heaven, they ne'er grew tired
    Of "little cares" or great.

But stronger grew the silken tie
    As sped their happy years;
And, with their treasures laid on high,
    They banished all their fears;
And, when at last they came to die,
    Were mourned with many tears.

If half they say of aunt be true,
    Her youthful charms were rare:
Her teeth were pearl, her eyes were blue,
    And auburn was her hair;
Her lip a rosebud bathed in dew;
    Her brow angelic, fair.

Never had maid a prettier hand,
    Or daintier foot, than she;
Nor rosier cheek had zephyr fanned
    Than hers, as all agree:
Her smile was like a seraph's bland,
    Her footstep light and free.

With thumb and finger, you would think
    Her waist that you could span.
She knew just when 'twould do to wink,
    Or smile, behind her fan:
Ay, hers were charms whose magic link
    'Twas hard to break, young man!

She dreamed of one — an idle dream —
    Whose look her fancy pleased:
Though but a dream, she did not seem
    By his indifference teased,
But clung to hope till hope's last gleam
    Had left her heart diseased.

When rouge supplants the artless rose,
    And life's a wintry sea,
None but an ancient maiden knows
    How pleasant it must be
To hear a gentleman propose,
    And see him bend the knee!

Ah! who can tell with what desire
  Aunt wished her years were stayed,
When youth had lost its subtle fire,
  And charms began to fade?
Yet ripening years saw her expire
  A lily in the shade.

And thus have all of that dear throng,
  Who cheered the ancestral hearth,
When I was young, and love was strong,
  And pure as flowers at birth,
Now trod the lonely way that's long,
  Nor more will visit earth.

When I return to earth's dull mould,
  Perhaps some kindred dear
Will smile to hear my foibles told,
  And think my portrait queer:
Nor matters it, if, when unrolled,
  Life's record still be clear.

THE REALM OF THOUGHT.

Around that realm there flames a wall
   No mortal foot hath scaled;
Nor through its gleaming turrets tall
   Hath tempest ever wailed.

A place of holy rest it seems,
   A palace built for souls, —
Great souls that realize their dreams
   'Mid light that boundless rolls;

Great souls that here have nobly wrought
   Their task, transferred at last,
There to partake, where truth is taught,
   An infinite repast.

THE MUSIC OF THE RAIN.

Now falling, falling from the sky,
    There comes a pleasant strain,
That lights with joy the floweret's eye, —
    The music of the rain.

And falling, falling on the roof,
    And on the window-pane,
It breathes of love that needs no proof, —
    The music of the rain.

And falling, falling down in showers,
    It cheers the waving grain,
And gives delight to summer hours, —
    The music of the rain.

And falling, falling in its mirth,
    It wakes to life again
The fainting world of lovely birth, —
    The music of the rain.

And falling, falling sweet and low,
    It falls on hill and plain,
And speeds the rills that dancing flow, —
    The music of the rain.

And falling, falling from the eaves,
    It mingles its refrain
With his who waits to gather sheaves, —
    The music of the rain.

And falling, falling far and near,
    It never falls in vain:
Oh, welcome then, with heart sincere,
    The music of the rain!

ASPIRATION.

BE mine a faith and hope whose tendrils twine
With buds and blossoms in a land divine,
Where spring but flowers that drink the genial dew,
And greet the sainted soul with welcome true;
Perennial flowers, whose pensive grace untold
Proclaims the power of love that's manifold;
The love that flows from out the central heart
Of Life unseen, yet flowing doth impart
To life that's seen its own diviner charm
Of moral beauty, with its healing balm;
Perennial flowers, that bloom in heavenly light,
And, ever fragrant, climb from height to height,
Where, free to all, a viewless hand unbars
The gate that leads to mansions built of stars.

SHADOWS.

In truth, all things beneath the sky
    But shadows seem, —
Shadows that catch the dazzled eye,
Mere shadows swiftly gliding by,
    False as a dream.

And yet, though false, they often cheer
    Hours dark to me:
Yes, often mirrored in a tear
I see familiar faces dear,
    No more to be.

Still all are shadows, man or flower,
    Passing with time;
All, — e'en the mountain's unscaled tower,
That awes the earth with mystic power
    Lone and sublime.

And yet, of sainted loved ones meek,
    Shadows are cast

From skies that ne'er grow chill or bleak;
Shadows that seem, heart-touched, to speak
    Of years now past;

Shadows that stalk close at my side,
    Life-like as truth;
Shadows in which I still confide;
Shadows that dance on life's dark tide;
    Shadows of youth;

Shadows of nymphs that trod the vale,
    And culled its flowers;
Shadows that loved the stars to hail,
And paused to hear the brooklet's wail,
    In moonlit hours;

Shadows of joys flown long ago
    With happier days;
Shadows of hours I ne'er shall know;
Shadows of hopes no more to glow,
    Shorn of their rays;

Shadows of memories ever blest,
    Though pensive all;
Shadows that come at my behest,
With healing power to soothe my breast,
    Whate'er befall.

Ah me! how oft have shadows brought
    One message more
From realms of bliss to souls untaught,
Prophetic of the change that's wrought
    When life is o'er!

A VISION OF LIGHT.

When the Winter departs
  On his dark, stormy wing,
How divine the first flower
  That appears in the spring!

'Tis a vision of light,
  And it comes but to cheer
Winter's last lingering frown
  With a smile that is dear.

And with joy, from the cup
  Of the silvery dew,
It imbibes nectared sweets,
  Ever pure, fresh, and new,—

Timely food sent to earth
  From a fount in the sky
In response to the prayer
  Of a calm, lifted eye.

Thus the flower looks aloft
  To the stars of the night
With a faith that is pure,
  And a brow crowned with light.

Though its life be a dream,
  And its days but a few,
Yet, like saint, it has hope,
  With a love breathed for you.

O ye proud of the earth!
  From the flower meekly learn
How to live, how to die,
  And be blessed in return.

LAURA.

The moment his leave he had taken,
   She flew from the parlor in haste,
With her nerves like an aspen quite shaken;
   Yet the secret was much to her taste.
"Oh! what is the matter, my dear?"
   Cried the mother, all pale with affright;
And Laura began to look queer,
   And to stammer, while blushing outright: —

"Frank asked me — I did not expect it —
   The *question!* I thought I should faint!
Such an offer! — oh! can I reject it?
   'Tis enough to discourage a saint.
How shall I determine his case?
   'Tis true that I love him too well;
But they say I've a beautiful face,
   And you know I'm considered a belle.

"Besides, there are forty or more
   With whom it is pleasant to flirt;
And they all still profess to adore, —

Would kiss e'en the hem of my skirt.
I'm alarmed at the hazard I run;
  So distracted, I hardly can speak:
I'll tell him I thought him in fun
  When he calls for an answer next week.

"But I'm fearful that never will do:
  His manner was frank and sincere:
An answer that's candid is due;
  And yet it will cost me a tear.
Let me think — ah! I think I'll say '*No!*'
  With Harry I love to play chess;
Yet, my hand were I now to bestow,
  A fopling it never should bless.

"As to Frank, I will treat him the same,
  And perhaps I will wed him at last.
But, when I consider how tame
  Are the married, I'm stricken aghast,
And conclude in the girlhood of life
  That I'll still be a butterfly gay:
When I choose, I will then be a wife;
  Yet I might marry dozens to-day."

And thus, with a toss of her head,
  She made up her mind in a hurry.

"AND, LISPING, REPLIED TO HIM, 'YES.'"—Page 123.

Frank called, and began to look red;
  Yet Laura, although in a flurry,
Received him, of course, with a smile;
  Then talked of the last evening's rout:
But Frank, after listening awhile,
  Resolved to remove the last doubt.

But still she persisted in talking
  Of the rout, and the fashions, and dance;
While Frank, as he rose to be walking,
  Still lingered, half lost in a trance;
When, wreathing her lip to say *"No!"*
  Somehow, with a charming address,
She softened the word in its flow,
  And, lisping, replied to him, *"Yes!"*

SONG OF THE DIME.

Though but a dime, a simple dime,
    I run a bright career,
And have a voice whose silvery chime,
    Like music, wins the ear.

Where'er I go, I'm still received
    With ready, grasping hand:
The rich, the poor, and the bereaved
    My mission understand.

Yet ere I can my mission prove,
    Though never seeking rest,
The miser, with a miser's love,
    Oft locks me in his chest.

Imprisoned there I'm doomed to wait,
    Still sighing to be free,
Until the tyrant yields to fate,
    And heirs obtain the key.

SONG OF THE DIME.

In social circles, high and low,
   I have a wide, wide range;
And still am sought, as you may know,
   By those who seek for "change."

A changing life it is I lead;
   And, though grown old and thin,
I still remain a slave indeed,
   Nor favors hope to win.

In ways that seem at first but small,
   Large fortunes oft I spend;
Amass them too, when saving all
   I find a faithful friend.

Yet many an orphan's heart I cheer
   With stinted loaves of bread,
And oft illume the widow's tear
   In pensive silence shed.

And yet the widow, poor indeed,
   Oft casts me, as her mite,
In aid of those who still have need
   Of gospel truth and light.

And thus from hand to hand I go,
   And do what good I can:

Yet much I do, in idle show,
    For woman and for man;

Nor cease to learn from day to day,
    As I enact my part,
How few are they who care to weigh
    The motives of the heart.

THE AUTUMN LEAF.

In you, frail leaf,
The lone and last on yonder tree,
Methinks, revealed, I clearly see
The life that's pure, — its harmony
    And golden sheaf.

And, though you wear
A pensive look, I still can trace
A saintly smile upon your face,
Betokening faith, — a work of grace
    That cheers despair.

To life's last bound,
Though tremulous has been your flight,
Still you have won a crown that's bright,
And, clad in gems, oft danced at night
    A giddy round, —

Danced to the sigh
Of zephyr's lute, 'mid summer air;

Nor dreamed that you were doomed to share
A frosty kiss, so calm and fair
    Appeared the sky.

But now, grown old,
'Tis yours to fall as fell your peers,
And mingle with the dust of seers;
Yet live again, and in far years
    New charms unfold.

'Twas but the breath
Of vernal hours that quickened you:
'Tis but a breath divine and true
That quickens man, and will renew
    His life in death.

LAYING THE CORNER-STONE.

[WRITTEN BY REQUEST.]

FATHER of light, enthroned on high,
    Thine is an ever-watchful care
O'er all who dwell beneath the sky,
    And thine an ear that heareth prayer.

To thee we here with willing hand,
    And cheerful hearts allied as one,
A temple rear to bless our land,
    And reverent lay the corner-stone.

'Tis here that we our vows will pay
    As fleeting roll our earthly years;
And, led by faith that points the way,
    Ne'er yield our hopes to doubting fears.

'Tis here that we will speak thy love,
    And sing thy praise in sacred song,
Invoke the spirit of the dove,
    And still in faith and hope grow strong.

And here to thee our hearts still give,
    And wait until from earth and strife
Thy voice shall bid us rise and live,
    Heirs of a purer, better life.

INSCRUTABLE.

Old Ocean, source of mystic power,
   I love thy solemn hymn,
The hollowed murmurs of thy lip,
   And saddened memories dim,
Yet shrink to meet thy terrors grim.

Nor marvel that thine own dark waves
   Refuse to give thee rest;
For thine are dark, mysterious deeds,
   Born of a troubled breast,
Still unatoned and unconfessed.

And yet methinks kind sympathies
   With human hearts are thine;
A wish to soothe the wail of grief, —
   The grief that's ever mine
For her whose form thy depths enshrine.

EVER VAIN.

EVER vain the pursuit
After pleasures that fly,
And bequeath but a sigh,
With a tear in our eye:
   Ashes the fruit!

Ever vain the pursuit,
Amid dreams that entrance,
After phantoms that dance,
After fame, — a mere chance:
   Ashes the fruit!

Ever vain the pursuit,
Amid grief from the first,
After bubbles that burst,
After treasures accursed:
   Ashes the fruit!

TACIT LANGUAGE.

WHEN eye for eye is glancing,
   Oft deep emotions rise,
Intwined with thoughts entrancing
   Whose memory never dies.

When sigh for sigh is heaving,
   Oft joy with grief is blent;
But, when fond hopes are leaving,
   How sad the heart's lament!

When smile for smile is lighting
   The fair angelic brow,
On lips that seem inviting
   Who would not seal his vow?

When tear for tear is flowing,
   Its light full oft reveals
A cherished love that's glowing,
   Which still the lip conceals.

When heart for heart is beating,
Its language must be true:
The heart cannot be cheating
That only beats for you.

A CONCEIT.

Old Father Time, with nod sublime,
   And hammer in his hand,
Proclaims aloud, as from a cloud,
   The sale of sea and land,
   With hammer in his hand.

Ask not for grace, but take your place,
   And hear him cry the sale:
He speaks in tones that shatter thrones,
   Nor lists to those who wail.
   Ah, hear him cry the sale!

Before him lies full many a prize
   In rich array displayed:
Yes, all that's dear to mortals here,
   Of life, its light and shade,
   In rich array displayed.

He breaks life's spell, nor grieves to sell
   Fond hopes to which we cling,—

Honor and fame, and wealth and name, —
  Vain things: what will they bring?
  Fond hopes to which we cling!

He spareth nought, not e'en a thought,
  Though beautiful and true,
But strikes down all, then flings a pall,
  And screens the world from view,
  The beautiful and true.

Nor does he wait at heaven's high gate,
  Nor does he shed a tear,
But breaks the bars, and smites the stars,
  And dark grows every sphere:
  Nor does he shed a tear,

But doomed now dies, 'neath blackened skies,
  Remembered nevermore;
And now, downcast, the silent Past
  In darkness hides her store, —
  Remembered nevermore.

LILIES.

If the stars are but footprints
  Where the angels have trod,
What are maidens but lilies
  In the garden of God?

What but daughters of light,
  Who in silence declare
Their devotion and love,
  With heads bowed in prayer?

But, if lilies "toil not,"
  How is it they weave
A wreath of sweet smiles,
  Yet deign to deceive?

While they flaunt, and seem gay,
  In their raiment of gold,
Why at heart are they sad
  With a "secret untold"?

HOME OF MY YOUTH.

A STRANGER in my native land,
  I none but strangers see;
Not one who seeks to grasp my hand,
  For none remember me.

Although received with chilling pride
  In this my native clime,
I have not now a heart to chide
  The changes wrought by time,

But still regard with tearful eye
  The shadows of the past,
The home of youth, whose magic sky,
  Though dimmed, is not o'ercast.

For I have seen beneath its roof
  Full many a happy day,
And heard from saintly lips the proof
  Of love that lasts for aye.

Yet nevermore shall I behold
   The years which now have flown,
Whose wings were wrought with threads of gold
   Bright as an angel's own.

But, yielding still to impulse strong
   That binds me in its band,
I turn to mountains loved so long,
   And kiss to them my hand;

And o'er paternal acres fair,
   That stretch beneath the sun,
Still trace the shadows gliding there,
   And mourn what time has done.

And yet I greet with joy the rill
   That flows from out the cave,
And winds its way adown the hill,
   Singing its ancient stave;

And bless the aged chestnut-tree,
   Where oft at earliest dawn
I gathered wealth, — then wealth to me, —
   Nor treat its gifts with scorn;

Nor shun the orchard, where of yore,
   Beneath an autumn sky,
I shared so oft the golden store
   That charmed my roving eye.

And thus, in passing o'er the lea,
   I pause at many a spot, —
Haunts which it gives me joy to see,
   Though changed is now my lot.

Ha! there's the vine, the wild grape-vine,
   In which I sat and swung
With her whose arm stole into mine
   In days when both were young.

Nor dreamed we then of happier hours,
   Nor happier have I seen;
For then life's path was strewn with flowers,
   And youth's bright sky serene.

And here once more old paths I tread
   In meadow, grove, and glade,
And pause 'neath elms whose leafy head
   Still casts a grateful shade.

HOME OF MY YOUTH.

In yonder glen the mountain-stream
   Propels the old mill-wheel;
And in good faith, as still would seem,
   The miller shares the meal.

Angling in depths to eddies wrought,
   Below the mill-dam's foam,
How oft the dainty trout I've caught,
   And borne in triumph home!

When Autumn with her golden hue
   Enriched the woodland's crown,
How oft with fatal aim and true
   I've brought the squirrel down;

Oft traced the pheasant to her glen,
   And set the subtle snare,
In which when caught, like luckless men,
   She dangled in the air!

Though skies may lower, the fitful gleams
   Of earlier, happier days
Still come to me like pleasant dreams,
   Tinged with celestial rays.

Yet, 'mid this vision of the past,
    Not one of all my race
Remains to cheer this lone and last
    Look at my native place.

And yet I love the sacred shrine
    Of olden memories dear,
And, lingering, dream of joys once mine,
    Though but a wanderer here;

In yonder churchyard trace the print
    Of names I honor still,
And from them take the warning hint
    Which time will soon fulfil.

Albeit familiar friends still live,
    Who seem to bless me yet,
And who to me a welcome give
    Which I can ne'er forget.

I mean the smiling brook that flows
    To music's silver tone,
The rock and hill, and sweet wild-rose,
    Whose love I'm proud to own.

Nor are they shadows dim to sight,
　Whose lips still breathe of woe,
But stanch old friends, whose hearts are right,
　True friends to me, I know.

None truer than the hills and plains,
　The brooklet, tree, and flower,
And birds that sing in happy strains,
　Unconscious of their power.

For Nature and her children speak
　In language that's divine,
And calmly teach me to be meek,
　And never to repine.

MORE SPACE.

Give Freedom space, more space;
　　Her proud domain extend;
But ne'er a step retrace;
　　Her blood-bought soil defend.

Space for the brave, more space,
　　O'er continent and sea:
Send forth Columbia's race,
　　Her sons of Liberty.

Space for her eaglets, space,
　　In other climes to soar, —
Soar in the sun's bright face,
　　Heralds from every shore.

Space for her banner, space,
　　On every breeze to float,
While tyrants trembling trace
　　Their fate not far remote.

Space for the free, more space!
   Ay, space for every man
Who dares to fill his place,
   Godlike, in Nature's plan.

Give Freedom space, more space;
   Her proud domain extend;
But ne'er a step retrace;
   For God is Freedom's friend.

AMONG THE HILLS.

WHEN Nature, with a skilful hand,
   Moulded to shape these billowy hills,
She clad in forests dark the land,
   And pencilled it with silver rills;
And, with a scarf of lovely blue,
   She bound the mountain's regal brow,
And touched it with a magic hue,
   Whose spell is flung around us now!

Here saintly forms before us pass,
   Arrayed in bright celestial beams,
Like visions seen in memory's glass,
   Whose smiles enchant our earthly dreams.
What though a Century has flown
   Since first our fathers hither came,
We see their faces — in our own —
   And kindle still their altar's flame!

And still 'mid shadows dimly trace,
   In every vale, hill-top, and glen,
The hearths they trod with manly grace,
   And still revere those godly men, —
The men who braved a savage foe,
   And prostrate laid the forest's pride;
Who thought it quite enough to know
   God's will, and take it for their guide.

Yet, 'mid the windings of the hills
   And silent shadows of the vales,
How sweet the music of the rills,
   That still the pilgrim's ear assails!
Though strangers in our Native Land,
   A welcome greets us without guile;
The hills extend a friendly hand,
   And valleys woo us with a smile.

Like old familiar friends they seem,
   The mystic pine, the mountain-peak,
The dreamy vale, and plaintive stream,
   That still to us in whispers speak.
Thus, pilgrim-like, we come, and glean
   The golden memories treasured here,
Yet feel that time can never wean
   Our hearts from scenes so fair and dear!

Beneath these same o'erarching skies
   Once more we look, with pure delight,
On sunny spots that charmed our eyes,
   And sportive fields that tried our might.
Oh, happy days! when we were young,
   When o'er these hills we trod the way,
Blithe as the morning lark that sung,
   In daisied meads, his roundelay!

Even yet, like fairy-land, appear
   The shelving rock and haunted glade,
And chestnut-groves to childhood dear,
   Where oft our footsteps we delayed.
But where are now the favorite few,
   Who shared, amid these kindred hills,
Our youthful sports and friendships true,
   Nor dreamed of life's impending ills?

In boundless realms beyond the stars,
   Theirs now are skies of holier light,
Where Truth her gate of pearl unbars,
   And blissful scenes regale the sight!—
God bless the land that gave us birth,
   Her many sons and daughters fair,
The dearest land of all the earth,
   Where first we breathed the mountain air'

FREEDOM.

I.

AH! who recalls the dark, unhallowed deeds
Which mark the sterner ages long gone by,
Nor starts at wrongs o'er which the heart still bleeds
When despots reigned, and bade their victims die,
And vainly flowed the tear from Pity's eye?
Though ours an age that's brighter, happier far,
Yet half mankind still bow, they know not why,
To sceptred power, or creeds they dare not mar;
Nor yet perceive the light that beams from Freedom's
    star.

II.

But why despair. There lives a spark divine
Within man's breast, surviving earth and tears;
And, where the moral virtues rear their shrine,
There heart to heart the social tie endears;
While Hope, whose star illumes the coming years,
Inspires with loftier aims and nobler zeal
Man's faith in man, and dissipates his fears,

And nerves his arm to strike 'mid clashing steel
For God and Truth, though empires to their centres
    reel.

III.

With smiling brow, and lip that breathed of peace,
From Eden's sheltering bowers nymph-like she
    came,
Nor found a genial clime, until in Greece
She there of yore acquired a glorious name, —
Freedom, whose pilgrimage is still of fame,
And 'neath whose banner heroes fought and bled,
Hurling the tyrants down to dust and shame
Who scourged the land in which the Arts were bred,
The land where still enshrined repose the mighty
    dead!

IV.

In that illustrious age when Athens shone,
And men the powers of earth and air adored,
There breathed a martial spirit now unknown;
And long, with unclipped wing, that spirit soared,
While human breasts with high resolves were stored,
And valiant deeds were done of great renown;
An age in which mankind preferred the sword,
And heroes strove to cleave stern heroes down,
Nor yet appeased the gods, who swayed by smile or
    frown.

V.

Then came an age as sparkling as its wine,
With mysteries which took the form of creeds,
And vows were paid at many an honored shrine,
While passion swayed the heart, and moral weeds,
Like noxious plants that broadcast sow their seeds,
Struck deep in genial soil, and ranklier grew;
Yet gods conversed with men, and Faith, that heeds
The marvellous, believed, howe'er untrue,
The dark responses which from unseen lips she drew.

VI.

Temples, from heights revered, o'erlooked the plain;
And patient Art, endowed with magic powers,
Gave unto Parian marble life and brain,
And sympathies which link the circling hours
Of time with classic beauty and with flowers;
Symbols which still attract our wondering eyes,
And still recall the listening groves and bowers
Where sages calmly walked in humble guise,
And held discourse with youth, and taught them to
  be wise.

VII.

And thus devout the philosophic Greek,
Who loved his templed hills and sunny vales,

Bequeathed to man, with spirit ever meek,
Doctrines sublime whose logic still entails
Its wealth, — a power that will, till blight assails
The earth, expand, and chasten human thought;
And yet how saddening were the hopeless wails
Uttered of old, when cruel deeds were wrought,
And tyrants gave command, and faith was sold and
    bought!

VIII.

Yet he who aimed at empire ne'er had dreamed,
When Rome's foundations were by him begun,
What lasting glory o'er him distant streamed
The while his warlike deeds were nobly done,
And stratagem the Sabine women won;
But when the city from her throne of hills
Beheld her fire-eyed eagles pierce the sun,
She seized on power that does whate'er it wills,
Nor kept her plighted faith, nor heeded human ills.

IX.

Still, in her better days, stern men were bred, —
Patriots who loved their country but too well,
And who unawed the flame of Freedom fed,
Till luxury and vice, with conquering spell,
Crept in, and fearful woes the state befell.

And yet the Eternal City lives, though shorn
Of ancient power, her name and fame to tell;
While 'mid her ruins shadows stalk forlorn,
And point at her degenerate sons with silent scorn.

X.

Alas! with all his pride and pomp and power,
The law of love nor Greek nor Roman knew:
Though martial glory crowned his triumph hour
'Mid trophies which attracted public view,
Though oft proclaimed a hero brave and true,
'Twas not enough; for his ambition's aim
Still fired his soul, as still the sword he drew;
And thus led on by that enchantress, Fame,
He sought to rank with gods, and craved a deathless name.

XI.

Freedom, whose cradle was the fearful storm,
As ages rolled, and darkness slow retired,
Maintained her faith, and, with affections warm,
Became at length of holier truths inspired,
And, clad in sacred armor, never tired,
But still, with frenzied eye and proud disdain,
Repelled her foes, and won a fame desired;
Nor from her shield erased the crimson stain,
But wide, and wider still, extended her domain.

XII.

And men grew wiser, better, as the flame
On Freedom's altar burned with clearer light;
And though dark years with darker errors came,
And fierce crusades with hate and venomed spite,
Though many a hero, mail-clad, fell in fight,
Yet Christian temples rose to bless the land,
While truth prevailed by force of moral might;
And, as the slumbering fires of faith were fanned,
E'en mitred priest at last relaxed his grasping hand.

XIII.

And moral heroes, weaned from mystic fear,
Flung off disguise, and strove with iron will
Their favorite creeds to herald far and near:
Yet strife begat but strife, with woes that chill
The manliest heart, 'mid scenes of glen and hill,
Where many a martyr, rash in conflict, fell,
And tinged with crimson flowed the mountain rill;
And where, 'mid desolation's brooding spell,
The spirit of the past, still ruthless, seems to dwell.

XIV.

'Twas thus, in proudest lands of earlier time,
When Freedom held at best imperfect sway,

That seeds were sown, which yet in every clime
Will spring to life as dawns the genial day,
When kings retire, and slavish creeds give way.
But when from Europe sailed her daring son,
Who sought and found in all its wild array
A Western world, how great the blessing won!
How great in years which yet shall in their circles run!

XV.

What though in later times the queenly isle,
That jealous mistress of the treasured sea,
Assumed an unrelenting power the while,
And bade her subjects bend a suppliant knee;
What though she did not leave opinions free:
There lived stern men e'en then, an honest few,
Who, taught by conscience, ever scorned to be
The dupes of royal pride; their rights they knew,
And, knowing them, remained to God and Freedom true.

XVI.

The Puritans, so called with meaning sneer,
Had struggled long and daringly, though vain,
Against the sceptre's scourge: nor ceased they here;
For Hope had flung her rainbow o'er the main,
And pointed to a land without a stain.
But still the pure affections of the heart

Endeared to them the mountain and the plain,
Their native clime, from which 'twas hard to part,
And leave their fathers' graves for wilds where terrors
    start.

XVII.

Yet when relentless wrong hath nerved the arm,
And stirred the soul, and waked the spirit there,
Men break their chains; nor can the tyrant calm
The rising storm, nor curb the brave who dare
Defend their dearest rights with bosoms bare.
How blest the world when tyranny shall yield
To stern reform, and all the nations share
A purer faith, and, trusting in the shield
Of virtue, see a manhood nobler yet revealed!

XVIII.

The Pilgrims now convened on ocean's strand,
And knelt to Heaven, yet lingered long to gaze
On friends and skies they loved, like Israel's band
Whose pathway was the sea in ancient days.
The parting hour had come: beneath the blaze
Of autumn's sun they bade a last farewell
To Britain's isle, and launched without amaze
Upon the billowy deep where dangers dwell,
And spread their sails to winds that sighed o'er
    ocean's swell.

XIX.

Westward the star of empire led the way,
Destined to glow within a broader sky,
And flash with light which yet shall fling its ray
Afar o'er earth's domain where shadows lie,
Inspiring hope and joy that will not die.
Yes, with a faith which gave them faith in man,
Heroes upon that star now fixed their eye,
And in the future saw the God-like plan
Which God himself had traced, whose truth inspired the van.

XX.

Hope gave them cheer, and "waved her golden hair."
Onward the voyagers ploughed the trackless sea,
'Mid storm and tempest and the lightning's glare,
Resolved to bend to none but God the knee.
And after many days they joyed to see
Columbia's hills; nor yielded to the shock
When woodlands rang with shouts of savage glee;
But calm and trustful still that Pilgrim flock
Now disembarked, and consecrated Plymouth Rock;

XXI.

The rock that's firmly planted by the sea,
Prescribing bounds where proudest waves are stayed;

The landmark which was set to liberty
When earth's foundations broad and deep were laid;
The rock on which erst stepped the Pilgrim maid [8]
Who led the way with smiles that ever cheer;
The spot that's guarded still by Freedom's blade;
Where oft the patriot drops a grateful tear,
And breathes the honored names of those who slumber
near, —

XXII.

Names that will live when centuries depart,
And still in moral virtue faith inspire,
And back to many a patriot's throbbing heart
Respond with balmy lip, as child to sire,
Waking within the soul the hallowed fire
That ever prompts the brave, who dare reclaim
Their Heaven-born rights, despite the tyrant's ire.
'Twas here the Pilgrims reared with purest aim
Altars to God, and lit them up with Freedom's flame.

XXIII.

Though girt with forests and a mountain chain
Whose slopes and glens, and secret caverns dark,
Had ever been the red man's wild domain,
The Pilgrims clung to hope's expiring spark,
And struggled with their foes, and set the mark

Of empire there on Ocean's circling strand,
And, like the chosen few who left the ark,
Went forth to scatter blessings through the land,
And rear the tree of Liberty with fostering hand.

XXIV.

When Freedom, plumed for glory's bright career,
Had been restrained, there woke a quenchless flame;
And men stood forth, unawed by taunt or sneer,
Who sought the battle-field, and won a name
That will not die, — a proud, immortal fame.
Dread days! when rallying trump and drum were heard,
And traitors bore, like Cain, the mark of shame
Upon their brows; when Britain's ire was stirred,
And e'en the patriot's hope seemed hopelessly deferred.

XXV.

Yet sentiments that flashed from patriot pen
Startled the world, and vexed the royal ear,
And, like a message sent from Heaven to men,
Illumed in eyes, unused to weep, the tear;
The immortal scroll, which freemen still revere,
And all mankind respect, — a trust that's thine
And mine: betray it not, nor yield to fear,

But still make Freedom's cause a cause divine,
And ever pure shall burn the flame that lights her
    shrine.

XXVI.

'Twas in those days that men of iron nerve
Proved to the world their courage and their worth;
And they were men whom threats nor gold could
    swerve
From duty, — Nature's noblemen by birth, —
Who in defence of life and cherished hearth,
And altars burning bright with sacred fires,
Poured out their blood upon the crimsoned earth,
A free libation to their high desires,
And love of right, which in the true heart ne'er
    expires.

XXVII.

And though but few, yet, resolute and strong,
Our banded sires withstood the invading foe,
And, 'neath their country's banner, struggled long,
Led on through varied scenes of blood and woe,
'Mid battle-smoke and cannon's fiery glow,
By him whose gallant deeds were ne'er outdone,
And who at Yorktown struck the final blow:
Glorious as great the triumph which was won
For man, for freedom, and the land of Washington!

"And who at Yorktown struck the final blow." — Page 170.

XXVIII.

For human weal or woe, sublime the trust
Reposed in those who rule our favored land.
And yet temptations, such as spring from lust
Of power, or love of fame, how few withstand!
How few whose virtues may not be unmanned!
But still there's hope in Freedom's sacred cause,
While firmly leagued the sisterhood shall stand,
And men bear sway who seek not vain applause,
Nor yield to sordid aims, but dare maintain the laws.

XXIX.

In schools of learning scattered far and wide,
And cherished fanes that skyward lift their spires,
In zeal for truth that's based on virtue's pride,
In brotherhood, and love, and pure desires,
And generous hearts that burn with Freedom's fires,
Consist our country's hope and future weal;
And, while we bless the memory of our sires,
For earth's oppressed still let us kindly feel,
And speed the day when none to tyrant power shall kneel.

OLD FOLKS' FESTIVAL.

Still pilgrims in a favored land,
  Who long have lingered on the way,
How blest to meet and grasp the hand,
  And crown with joy our festive day ! —

And tell of years whose scenes return,
  Like shadows on our pathway cast;
And catch, from living lips that burn,
  The fleeting memories of the past.

And while we trace from whence we sprung,
  And early friendships fain renew,
Still let us dream that we are young,
  And, though a dream, believe it true !

Nor days forget when first we heard
  Life's battle-cry, and sought the field;
When lofty aims our bosoms stirred,
  And faith had armed us with her shield.

'Twas courage, then, with youthful zeal,
   That led us onward, flushed with pride;
'Tis years, now ripe, that make us feel
   How swiftly glides life's ebbing tide!

Yet while we here prolong our stay,
   We'll keep our pledge of love and truth;
And when we pass the darkened way,
   Ascend and share immortal youth!

NOTES.

NOTES.

Note 1. — Page 7.

"Breathes of the past, 'tis consecrated ground."

Mount Vernon, consecrated as the home of Washington, is pleasantly situated in the county of Fairfax, Virginia, on the south bank of the Potomac, and has an elevation of two hundred feet above the surface of the river, which at this point is two miles wide.

The old family mansion, which crowns the hill, was originally built by Washington's uncle, who gave it the name of "Mount Vernon" in honor of Admiral Vernon, under whom he had served in the British navy.

Note 2. — Page 8.

"Though but a lowly shrine."

The object of the most intense interest to visitors, at Mount Vernon is, of course, the tomb of Washington. It is situated in a lovely retreat on the hillside, and, though not seen from the river, is suddenly disclosed to view as you ascend the hill from the landing.

This retired yet hallowed spot is sprinkled with wild flowers and shaded by the dark cedar and the stately oak, and was selected, it is said, by Washington himself, for the purpose to which it has been appropriated. The tomb is of moderate dimensions and of plain exterior, constructed of brick, with an iron door of open-work, through which you can see in the interior two marble sarcophagi arranged side by side, one of which contains the remains of George Washington, and the other those of Martha his wife.

Note 3. — Page 8.

"But turn where stands the hall
In which the chieftain dwelt of yore."

The Mount-Vernon estate still remains much as it was in the days of Washington. With a view to its preservation, it has been purchased by an association. It should belong to the nation.

Note 4. — Page 12.

"While tears with magic power
In silence fell, like dewdrops on the flower."

Speaking of Lafayette's visit in 1824 to the tomb of Washington, Mr. Lavasseur, who was present, says in his correspondence, that Lafayette descended alone into the vault, and, in a few minutes after, re-appeared with his eyes overflowing with tears. This occurred at the old tomb from which the remains were afterwards removed to the new tomb where they now rest.

Note 5. — Page 14.

"Flung back from hill to hill with wild delight!"

Mr. Sparks, in his "Life of Washington," remarks in reference to the success of the American arms at the battle of Trenton, that "the despondency which had weighed heavily on the minds of the people was dispelled as by a charm, the martial spirit revived, and a new animation infused into the public councils."

Note 6. — Page 16.

"But now, from proffered kingly crown,
With scorn he turned away."

A short time before the American army was disbanded at the close of the Revolution, a colonel in the service, "of a highly respectable character, and somewhat advanced in age," as the agent of those engaged in the scheme, communicated to Gen. Washington a very flattering proposal to permit himself to be made king over the American people; to which the general indignantly replied in the following characteristic letter, as noble and patriotic in sentiment as it is beautiful in style: —

NEWBURG, 22 May, 1782.

Sir, — With a mixture of great surprise and astonishment, I have read with attention the sentiments you have submitted to my perusal. Be assured, sir, no occurrence in the course of the war has given me more painful sensations than your information of there being such ideas existing in the army as you have expressed, and which I must view with abhorrence, and reprehend with severity. For the present, the communication of them will rest in my own bosom, unless some further agitation of the matter shall make a disclosure necessary.

I am at a loss to conceive what part of my conduct could have given encouragement to an address which to me seems big with the greatest mischiefs that can befall my country. If I am not deceived in the knowledge of myself, you could not have found a person to whom your schemes are more disagreeable. At the same time, in justice to my own feelings, I must add, that no man possesses a more sincere wish to see ample justice done to the army than I do; and as far as my power and influence, in a constitutional way, extend, they shall be employed to the utmost of my abilities to effect it, should there be any occasion. Let me conjure you, then, if you have any regard for your country, concern for yourself or posterity, or respect for me, to banish these thoughts from your mind, and never communicate, as from yourself or any one else, a sentiment of the like nature.

I am, sir, &c.,
GEORGE WASHINGTON.

Note 7. — Page 17.
"How vain the lofty tower."

Alluding to the Washington Monument in the city of Washington.

Note 8. — Page 168.
"The rock on which erst stepped the Pilgrim maid."

Dr. Thacher, in his "History of the Town of Plymouth," states that, "'The Mayflower' having arrived in the harbor from Cape Cod, Mary Chilton entered the first landing boat, and, looking forward, exclaimed, 'I will be the first to step on that rock!' Accordingly, when the boat approached, Mary Chilton was permitted to be the first from the boat who appeared on the rock."

SELECT POEMS.

BY HARVEY RICE.

NOTICES OF THE PRESS.

"'SELECT POEMS,' recently published by Lee & Shepard, Boston, pp. 174, 12mo, are from the pen of Hon. Harvey Rice of Cleveland, O., and author of 'Nature and Culture,' published by the same firm in 1875, and which contained several essays on those subjects worthy of the deepest consideration.

"In the volume now before us, the same love and admiration of all things good, noble, patriotic, and beautiful, are to be observed; and we wish that some of our magazine-writers would take pattern by the plain, almost severe, Saxon verbiage in which the deepest thought and most vivid fancy find expression." — *Journal of Commerce, Boston.*

"A second edition indicates the public estimate of these piquant, graceful, and, in many regards, beautiful creations. We still think that 'Unwritten Music' rightfully fills the first place. It is simply exquisite." — *Christian Leader, Boston.*

"Among the best of the long poems are 'The Mystery of Life,' 'Mount Vernon,' 'Ancestral Portraits,' 'Home of my Youth,' and 'Freedom.' The short poems are all good, some of them being perfect gems." — *Eastern Argus, Portland, Me.*

"A collection of original poems, all of which are pleasing in structure, pure and elevated in sentiment, vigorous and refined in diction, and faultless in numbers. The religion is that of the natural man, the morality that of works, the sympathy tender, and the wit general. The lovers of good poetry will relish the feast." — *Epis. Recorder, Phil.*

"Mr. Rice writes true poetry." — *New-York Methodist.*

LEE AND SHEPARD, PUBLISHERS.

www.ingramcontent.com/pod-product-compliance
Lightning Source LLC
Chambersburg PA
CBHW032132160426
43197CB00008B/614